The Practical Guide to Managing Event Venues

This is a short, accessible and practical guide to running venues which are in the business of hosting events. Using honest guidance peppered with the author's real-life situational anecdotes to contextualise the topics, the book is logically structured around the key stages of event management: pre-event, onsite and post-event. Topics covered include developing the client relationship, marketing, financial accountability, risk, interdepartmental communication, onsite procedures and post-event evaluation. This is a fundamental resource for all event management and hospitality students. It is also a book for anybody who manages a venue or is a venue event manager. *The Practical Guide to Managing Event Venues* makes the business of venue management appealing, understandable and achievable.

Philip Berners has been the event manager at high-profile venues, including the London Hippodrome, Camden Palace and Thorpe Park. He has also organised events in a range of venues in the UK, Poland, Portugal and Italy. His knowledge of using venues for events extends to public parks, royal parks, conference centres, nightclubs, hotels, restaurants, sports centres, exhibition halls, country houses and disused warehouses. He is currently lecturer and course coordinator for the BA Hons Events Management programme at the Edge Hotel School, University of Essex, UK.

The Practical Guide to Managing Event Venues

Philip Berners

Routledge
Taylor & Francis Group
LONDON AND NEW YORK

First published 2019
by Routledge
2 Park Square, Milton Park, Abingdon, Oxon OX14 4RN

and by Routledge
711 Third Avenue, New York, NY 10017

Routledge is an imprint of the Taylor & Francis Group, an informa business

© 2019 Philip Berners
Section 11.1 'Management of catering outlets' © Jennifer Kaye
Chapter 13 (to end of section 13.4) © Adrian Martin
Case Study 'A wedding in Tuscany' © Dimitri Lera

The right of Philip Berners to be identified as author of this work has been asserted by him in accordance with sections 77 and 78 of the Copyright, Designs and Patents Act 1988.

All rights reserved. No part of this book may be reprinted or reproduced or utilised in any form or by any electronic, mechanical, or other means, now known or hereafter invented, including photocopying and recording, or in any information storage or retrieval system, without permission in writing from the publishers.

Trademark notice: Product or corporate names may be trademarks or registered trademarks, and are used only for identification and explanation without intent to infringe.

British Library Cataloguing-in-Publication Data
A catalogue record for this book is available from the British Library

Library of Congress Cataloging-in-Publication Data
A catalog record has been requested for this book

ISBN: 978-1-138-48639-3 (hbk)
ISBN: 978-1-138-48640-9 (pbk)
ISBN: 978-1-351-04559-9 (ebk)

Typeset in Iowan Old Style
by codeMantra

Contents

List of contributors ix
Acknowledgements x

PART I
The management of event venues 1

1 **What is a venue?** 3
   1.1 Definition of venue 3
   1.2 Types of venue 3
   1.3 The demand for unusual venues 7

2 **The Berners hierarchy of event needs** 8

3 **Hotels as venues for events** 11
   3.1 How hotels can recapture events business 13

4 **Venue reputation** 18
   4.1 History of a venue 20
   4.2 Testimonials 20
   4.3 Client portfolio 21
   4.4 Online reviews 21
   4.5 By types of events 22
   4.6 Referrals by word of mouth 22
   4.7 View the venue – meet the team 23

5	**Events as a source of income**		24
	5.1 Venues with events as the primary source of income		24
	5.2 Venues with events as their secondary source of income		25
6	**Venue professionalism**		29
	6.1 What makes a 'good' venue		34
	6.2 Venue show-round		38
7	**The need to meet expectations**		41
8	**Venue culture change**		43
	8.1 The need for good communication		44
	8.2 Interdepartmental communication		46
	8.3 The communication process for venues		52
9	**The Berners one-person management structure**		55
	9.1 Client relationship		57
	9.2 Receiving information		58
	9.3 Disseminating information		58
	9.4 Onsite event management		58
10	**The role of the venue**		63
11	**Procuring external services**		74
	11.1 Management of catering outlets		77
	11.2 Guiding the client		87
12	**Winning business and retaining clients**		91
	12.1 Reactive marketing		91
	12.2 Proactive marketing		96
	12.3 Winning events business		98
	12.4 Tendering		99
	12.5 Pitching		100
	12.6 Repeat business		102
13	**Budgeting for events**		105
	13.1 Where budgets come from		106
	13.2 How to create a budget		109
	13.3 How budgets are developed		112
	13.4 Return on investment (ROI)		114
	13.5 Venue hire fee		118

14	Guests at venues	**120**
	14.1 Personal safety of guests	120
	14.2 Risk management	122
	14.3 Common mistakes of venues	124

PART II
Event procedures for venues **133**

15	Enquiry handling	**135**
	15.1 Receiving the enquiry	138
	15.2 Date conflict	138
	15.3 Enquiry file procedure	140
16	Show-round procedure	**142**
17	Confirmation and contract procedure	**146**
	17.1 Venue contract (Appendix II)	146
18	Lead-in procedure	**154**
19	Client file procedure	**158**
20	Client relationship procedures	**160**
21	Event schedule/function sheet (Appendix III)	**163**
22	Operational procedures	**167**
23	Get-in and set-up procedure	**171**
	23.1 Set-up	172
24	Rehearsal procedure	**173**
25	During-event procedures	**175**
	25.1 Security briefing	176
	25.2 Final walk-round	176
	25.3 Opening the doors	178
	25.4 Checking	179
	25.5 Catering	180
	25.6 Closing	181
26	De-rig procedure	**183**

PART III
Post-event procedures — 185

27 Post-event procedures — 187
  27.1 Debriefs — 189
  27.2 Guest satisfaction evaluation — 192
  27.3 Problem solving — 194
  27.4 Final report (Appendix IV) — 198

28 Case studies — 201
  Case study 1 by Philip Berners: the London Hippodrome — 201
  Case study 2 by Philip Berners: Thorpe Park — 203
  Case study 3 by Dimitri Lera: a wedding in Tuscany — 205

Appendix
  I   Event forecast — 209
  II Venue contract — 211
  III Function sheet/event schedule — 222
  IV Final report — 224

Glossary — 227
Index — 229

Contributors

Jennifer Kaye has been working in higher education since 2010 and is currently a hotel and events lecturer at the Edge Hotel School in Essex. Jenny taught a range of hospitality, business and management subjects in her previous employment as Programme Leader at University Centre Colchester and graduated with an MBA in 2017. With over 22 years of industry experience, Jenny has worked within a number of roles in the hospitality and events industries including leading hotel chains, within contract events and sports stadia, and she continues to work in the sector to ensure that her subject knowledge is current.

Dimitri Lera is an alumnus of the École Hôtelière de Lausanne and began his international managerial career at the age of 20 as a restaurant manager in Bournemouth. At 27 he was put in charge of the opening of the first ever river cruise ship operating in Italy. By 30 he was Deputy Hotel Director on the Silver Sea, achieving the award of 'most luxurious ship' by Condé. In recent years, and after managing one of London's best established Italian restaurants in Chelsea, Dimitri's ambition to teach and his passion for hospitality led him to the position of lecturer at the Edge Hotel School at the University of Essex. Dimitri is also passionate about languages, capable of conversing in seven languages, and holds an MFL PGCE and is close to completion of his MA.

Adrian Martin graduated with a Degree and Master's in Hotel and Catering Management from Manchester University before working for Thistle Hotels in London, Bath, Bristol and Bedford. At just 24, he became General Manager of a hotel in Bournemouth and managed to save it from bankruptcy to run it for a further six years. His ambition to teach meant he left the trade and taught at Bournemouth College, before being promoted to Head of School. In 2014 he took what he describes as 'the opportunity of a lifetime' to become Vice Principal of the Edge Hotel School, the UK's first Hotel School, where degree students work in an operational 4* hotel on campus as part of their course.

Acknowledgements

I wish to thank Olaf Olenski for support with compiling this second book in the series. I also extend my gratitude to Jenny Kaye, Dimitri Lera and Adrian Martin for contributing to this book.

Philip Berners
2018

PART I

The management of event venues

Chapter 1

What is a venue?

1.1 Definition of venue

In my first book of this series, *The Practical Guide to Organising Events,* I defined an event as ***any live happening***.

A **venue** is where a live happening takes place.

If the live happening is not an accident or incident, but is planned (events management is the planning of live happenings), then the venue is an *event venue* – even if it is used for a one-off event.

1.2 Types of venue

Now we understand what a venue is, we can identify various types of venue where events take place.

1.2.1 Dedicated venues

A dedicated venue is a place constructed for the purpose of staging or hosting events – we may call this type of venue a *purpose-built* venue.

This type of venue would usually be built specifically for a certain type of event, such as a conference centre for hosting conferences, or a sports stadium for hosting sporting events.

4 THE MANAGEMENT OF EVENT VENUES

Being a venue built for purpose, the architect would design the facility specifically for the needs of that type of event. For example:

Type of venue	Design features
Conference centre	Large foyers for delegate registration
	Main conference hall
	Breakout meeting rooms
	Stage
	Sound, lighting and projection facilities
	Translation booths
	Multiple bars
	Buffet/dining areas

Otherwise, it could be a purpose-built multi-purpose venue, such as modern-day sports stadia which are now designed to facilitate the business of all events, not just sporting. Nowadays, a sports stadium will incorporate conference facilities, banqueting suites and nightclubs.

1.2.2 Non-dedicated venues

This type of venue is not built for the purpose of events. This could be an art gallery, nightclub, museum, library or any other building that could host an event due to its size, location, facilities or interesting architecture, but the primary purpose of the building is not events.

Venues that are not built for the purpose of events will most often have a core business that is not events driven. In such venues, their events business is secondary. These are 'part-time' event venues, then.

Within this category, could also be included pubs, bars and restaurants because their main purpose of business is that of retailing food and drink. Yet, most pubs host social events, such as quiz nights, live music, and New Year's Eve parties, and most restaurants host parties, wedding banquets and private dining rooms. Even so, this does not make them *dedicated* event venues.

An example of this type of venue would be the Natural History Museum in London – which, although was not constructed for the purpose of hosting events, but for housing and displaying museum exhibits – does host an extraordinary number of corporate parties, weddings, conferences, fashion shows, and filming. Its primary role as a museum means that this particular venue is open to the public every day from 10:00 until 17:30. Thus, the Natural History Museum hosts events as a secondary contribution to its core business. As with most such venues, the Natural History Museum splits its role to accommodate events outside its usual operating hours.

Even if a palace, castle or historic house were now purpose-run for events – as many are these days for weddings, team-building activities, small conferences – and events have become the primary income, it would be wrong to categorise this venue as being dedicated because it cannot be assumed that *all* palaces, castles and historic houses are run solely for the purpose of events. Besides, a palace, castle or historic house was not built for the *purpose* of events.

A non-dedicated event venue may also be a 'green-field' site, such as a public park hosting an open-air concert, funfair or festival.

Note: A 'green-field' site is not necessarily a parkland or grassy area, but is the generic term applied to a venue where limited or no facilities exist. Green-field sites can be empty buildings, disused factories, warehouses, car parks or anywhere where no facilities or services exist in situ. Indeed, in many cases, green-field sites do not have electricity, water, drainage or toilet facilities.

Where there are basic facilities, the venue would be termed as a 'brown-field' site.

Examples of dedicated and non-dedicated venues

Dedicated	Non-dedicated
Hotels	Green-field sites
Conference centres	Historic houses
Sports stadia	Museums
Banqueting halls	Public libraries
Exhibition halls	Castles
	Palaces
	Pubs, bars, restaurants
	Nightclubs
	Theatres
	Country house hotels

Examples of popular events held at non-dedicated venues

Chelsea Flower Show	held at	The Royal *Hospital* Chelsea
Hampton Court Flower Show	held at	Hampton Court *Palace*
The Route of Kings Concerts	held at	Hyde *Park*
The BAFTA Awards	held at	The Royal *Opera* House
The Hay Literary Festival	held at	*marquees* at Hay on Wye
Glastonbury Festival	held at	a working dairy *farm*

1.2.3 Unusual venues

There are certain venues that fall into the *unusual venue* category (otherwise referred to as *special venues*). These are places that can already be identified as non-dedicated venues, but also they would rarely host events or may never have hosted an event.

So, whereas the Natural History Museum in London is non-dedicated for events, it has become adept at hosting many events and has an events team; it has well-practiced events procedures; and it has a portfolio of trusted suppliers, such as technical providers and event catering companies. It is important to note here that an events team in a venue such as this would be experienced in client handling and events management.

The difference which makes an *unusual* venue, is a non-dedicated venue that does not have an events team because the premises are not usually used for events. Therefore, none of the staff would have events experience, the venue is not practiced in managing and handling events, and there would be no chain of trusted events suppliers.

The question may arise as to why a client would seek an unusual venue. It would be because the client wants somewhere *unusual* – somewhere that is unique, and where no other client has yet held an event.

Such unusual venues may be country houses, warehouses, private estates, disused buildings, barns, or any place of architectural interest.

1.3 The demand for unusual venues

In simple economic terms, demand drives need. Creativity is the new need. So, event clients have learnt to search for more exciting, more innovative and more interesting venues.

And, it is an upward spiral: the more adventurous a client is with choosing a venue one year, so their need is to be even more adventurous the following year.

This does not mean that if a venue is traditional or is a dedicated events venue it will lose out to unusual or non-dedicated venues. What it does mean is that *all* venues need to provide their clients and guests with a top-quality event experience. Otherwise, the venue – dedicated or otherwise – will lose business to its competitors. In today's event marketplace, where all buildings are potential venues, all other buildings are competitors.

So, achieving bookings through events is ever more an aggressive and increasingly competitive market. Venues have to try harder. They need to create their reputation for good event handling, and protect it. They require knowledgeable and trained events staff to attract and retain events business… And, so the events industry is self-regulating. It is evolving and getting better at it. There are qualifications in events management now – it has become a career!

Chapter 2

The Berners hierarchy of event needs

The demand for venues is driven for the following reasons, which we may call 'The Berners Hierarchy of Event Needs'.

1. A need to avoid traditional event venues, particularly hotels. In event circles, hotels represent lazy and boring events (this is discussed further in Chapter 3).

2. The need to excel the previous event. If the event occurs annually – a Christmas party or a yearly conference, say – the company or client will need to excel the previous year's event experience.

3. The need to outdo competitors. Where a company's competitor is providing an event for their clients, there is a need to outdo the competition.

4. To continue the need for newness, excitement, progression and growth. If a company is innovative, and is growing and improving, it will not want its events to remain staid and non-progressive.

5. The need to reflect the company's profile. Often, the client will seek a venue which reflects the company profile. So, a company that designs expensive contemporary furniture, say, would not choose to place their event in a rundown local hotel.

6. The need to entertain guests in a surprising and exciting environment. Another reflection of a company's dynamics, clients strive to project the core values of the business by choosing unusual venues for their events.

7   The need to generate word-of-mouth success. Clients need their event guests to be talking about a memorable event, and what a wonderful and exciting event they attended.

8   To provide the 'need' for guests to attend the event. A poorly attended event would be a negative reflection of a company's success. So, the venue needs to be exciting, interesting and otherwise inaccessible so as to help with the 'need to attend' factor. It also drives the need for guests to receive an invitation for next year's event, and confirm their attendance.

9   The need to add value to the event. An exciting and fascinating venue adds value to the guest experience.

10 The need to provide guests with a unique experience. Corporate event clients do not wish to follow trends – they wish to *set* trends.

11 The need to achieve press coverage. High-profile events tend to book unusual venues to heighten press interest and coverage.

AUTHOR'S VOICE BOX

Recently, a publishing company with offices in central London flew its sales team to Monaco for a two-day conference.

Clearly, there are many suitable venues in London, itself – within walking distance of the publisher's offices, certainly. If not in London, there are venues to choose throughout the UK.

Yet, the decision was taken to outlay the expense, fly the entire sales team to Monaco, have dinner at a beachside restaurant and play a few roulette chips at the famous Monte Carlo casino.

Why?

For the *experience*.

Over recent years, the events industry has noticeably shifted from traditional venues, to doing just about anything, just about anywhere.

This makes for exciting events and unbridled creativity, which is a good thing.

For event services providers and particularly for venues, the fact that events are no longer hidden in dedicated venues means it is boon time.

It has driven the growth of the events industry and related service providers: specialist event organisers, production companies, marquee suppliers, outside catering companies, furniture hire companies, mobile toilet facilities, electricity and water suppliers, decorators, stage hire, sound and lighting hire companies, crew and riggers, temporary fencing, security, logistics companies, transportation drivers ...

The emergence of events from the traditional venues has also opened opportunities for event management as a career choice. People are now more exposed to events, which inspires them to enter the business of events management.

The diversity of event venues also allows people to work with events in a variety of locations and a range of environments – museums, art galleries, shopping centres, palaces – whereas at one time event management was limited to dedicated venues – conference centres, sports stadia, or hotels.

One does not need to look for events or come across them by accident – they now happen everywhere.

Chapter 3

Hotels as venues for events

Some time ago, events were held only in hotels. In those days it was unthinkable to search for unusual venues because hotels have everything one needs for an event– banquet rooms, ballrooms, dance floors, furniture, technical facilities, bars, kitchens and catering, waiters and bar staff …

Hotels of good repute also have quality management who are experienced and trained. Hotel management courses predate events management courses by a long way, so most good hotels have qualified management, too.

And, hotels have dedicated departments for handling events – the 'conference and banqueting' (C&B) department.

Considering these attributes, why would an event client look outside the world of hotels that could facilitate the needs, and all in one place?

Well, hotels are *too* convenient, and this has become their downfall.

The one-size-fits-all nature of hotels to meet the needs of a range clients (a range of budgets; and a range of type of event, such as conference clients or banquet clients) means hotel décor is designed to be generic. This is why hotel banqueting and conference suites are notoriously bland and nondescript. These types of spaces do not allow for the creativity of events. For one thing, hotel event suites are most often low-ceilinged which prevents the creativity of events where height is needed for projection, fog machines, balloon nets, confetti canons, snow machines and lighting effects.

The all-in-one-place nature of hotels has created a problem, too. Because everything is available in situ, hotels can keep costs low because everything is onsite. A hotel does not have the costs of hiring in from third parties, and there are no hire or transportation costs. Because hotels own their facilities, they can either waive additional charges or choose how much to charge, according to each client's budget.

This has led to a perception in the events industry that if it is a low-budget event, get it into a hotel.

Event clients do not want to be seen as 'cheap', or that their budget is miserly. For this reason, clients are beginning to insist that their event is *not* placed in to a hotel.

It should be noted that in times of recession or financial crisis, keeping the event costs low can project a positive connotation.

There is another barrier to placing events in to hotels. The fact that a hotel has everything in-house means there is little or no ability for a specialist event organiser to make money from their client. Yes, an event organiser will charge an event management fee, but additional revenue is achieved through the creative elements. And, if an event organiser is using trusted and loyal suppliers such as technicians, florists, furniture hire or caterers, there is room for mark-up and commissions. If the hotel is providing it all, the event organiser loses the opportunities for additional revenue. For this reason, many specialist event organisers will avoid placing their clients in to hotels.

On top of all this, hotels are notorious for poaching event clients from event organisers. By nature and necessity, hotels deploy aggressive sales techniques to meet targets for bedroom sales and food and beverage sales. Events is just another department, and it has its targets to achieve, too. Internal (and external) benchmarking determines performance measurement key performance indicators which push departmental managers into aggressive sales techniques. So, a specialist event organiser will not always wish to introduce their client to a hotel where everything is provided – including a client account manager, probably. It is easy for a hotel to convince a client that the hotel can 'do it all', and everything is already here anyway, so why pay additionally for a specialist event organiser?

It may be seen from the above, that the problems with events in hotels are of their own making. It could be viewed that hotels have created their own barriers which prevent clients from booking their event into a hotel, or for an events specialist to take their client in to a hotel.

But, there is still need and demand for events in hotels – and always will there be.

Hotels of good repute do provide the comfort and certainty of consistent standards and quality, and experienced and qualified staff and management. They will most certainly be practised in client handling and events management as well.

Sometimes, the event budget will be restricted, thus it makes sense to take the event to a place that has most or all elements in situ. And, where a venue has everything available in-house, the logistics and effort is much simpler – wedding clients who are unfamiliar with organising an event, like hotels for this reason.

Or, the requirements of the event make a hotel the most suitable and relevant venue. A conference that requires theatre-style rows of chairs in a large auditorium, a range of breakout rooms for splinter meetings, and overnight accommodation for the delegates, would make a hotel the obvious choice.

In fact, hotels are the obvious choice for *any* type of event which requires overnight accommodation for guests.

The requirement for bedrooms brings us to the 'need' factor. And, largely it is the 'need' of the event which determines choosing a hotel for an event, not the want or desire to do so.

It is this 'need' that hotels are relying upon now that the trend for events is more creative and clients are asking for unusual venues instead of hotels.

It could be that hotels do not yet realise they have lost the 'desire' for events to be placed into this type of venue. Even if this *is* a realisation, they may not know how to get it back.

Note here that not all hotels are dedicated event venues. Those hotels that were not purpose-built, such as country houses that are now hotels, are non-dedicated venues.

3.1 How hotels can recapture events business

In times long past, hotels were places to sleep. But, hotels have evolved into diverse brand categories to meet the change in demand and need of guests: star rated; AA rated; budget; luxury; boutique; country house; resort hotels.

Diversification has even taken place within hotels and they now provide cafes, bistros, brasseries, fine dining restaurants, lounges, meeting places, conferences, banquets, weddings, awards ceremonies and other events. Even bedrooms are now diverse, including standard rooms, executive rooms, balcony rooms and suites.

Hotels have long been known for the add-ons to their accommodation service – diversifying the core business to provide revenue streams from other sources, such as food and drink, casinos, nightclubs, swimming pools, leisure facilities, meeting rooms, conference spaces and banqueting halls. All of which are extensions to the core business of providing a place to sleep.

One might argue with reason that a hotel is obliged to provide food and drink because hotel guests require breakfast and perhaps an evening meal. But, it is not uncommon to find hotels without dining facilities, but with a restaurant and bar adjacent which is also a non-residential offering. Anyway, the basic catering needs of guests now extends to offer a lobby bar, rooftop bar, wine bar, café, bistro *and* a la carte restaurant. Even celebrity chefs are putting their name to hotel restaurants so as to drive business into this diversification.

It was natural organic growth for events to become yet another extension of a hotel's offering, driven by demand. As already identified in this book, hotels have most event facilities in situ – kitchens, bars, cleaning staff, waiting staff, cloakrooms, toilets, and guest bedrooms for overnight stays, of course.

In countries with an undeveloped events industry, hotels may still be the main venues for hosting events. But, this will not last very long. Even in those markets, hotels are already experiencing the situation of no longer attracting creative events with high-end budgets. Soon, they will find themselves struggling to attract even the mainstay conferences, presentations and dinners – unless there is the need for bedrooms.

Developing markets follow the trends of developed markets, so this is not merely conjecture, but the evaluation of an industry trend.

The need to get away from the traditional event venue and provide guests with the *Berners hierarchy of event needs* (outlined in Chapter 2) is an ongoing driver for clients to search for venues other than hotels.

In turn, event clients are becoming more educated and experienced in how to approach and organise events in non-dedicated and unusual venues. Also, guests' expectations have risen as they have been exposed to the unlimited potential of attending more exciting and creative events.

The ongoing rejection of using hotels for events has gradually led to them falling out of fashion on the venues circuit. The attitude seems to be that hotels *were* once the way of hosting conferences, seminars, meetings and banquets.

But, there will always be demand for events in hotels. Bedrooms are often a factor in the requirements of an event client. But, the event's budget is always going to be a decisive factor when choosing the venue. Hotels have the ability to provide most of the standard needs of an event without additional expense and the cost of hire. Also, is the need for quality space in the right locations – and city centre hotels meet this need.

Many hotels occupy strategic locations in city centres, or picturesque rural locations, or at busy intersections. This is another reason for them to attract events business. Many hotels themselves are the local landmark, which makes for a recognisable location for an event and is easy for guests to find.

Reliability is a factor, too. There are no chains of event venues, but there are plenty of hotel chains. This enables an event organiser to know the levels of standards and services they will receive at a hotel within a particular chain, in whichever city or country the event takes place. If this is an international client or the event is to take place in various locations at home or abroad, the consistency of a hotel chain is invaluable. It also allows for the potential to negotiate the cost of a series of bookings.

Many hotels have managed to develop their brand to be synonymous with top-quality events. Both the Grosvenor House hotel and the Dorchester hotel on London's Park Lane are prime examples of this. Each hotel is a luxury-end establishment which also hosts events to the extent that these hotels are renowned event venues. If the event is at The Grosvenor House or The Dorchester, it will be a high-quality event because of the quality of hotel, the location … and budget.

The hotel industry is itself adapting to the shift in event demands. Most hotel chains have begun to identify the threat of competition from a closely related industry which has evolved rapidly and is having negative impacts on hotel levels of business. Here, is an example where an industry has diversified, devolved and is under threat. Hotels are a victim of their own success – what was once held within, is now an external beast with sharp teeth.

Waking up to this scenario – albeit slowly – hotels are offering incentives to corporate clients, such as club membership rewards and loyalty discounts.

Hotels also offer discounted accommodation if the event takes place in their banqueting rooms. Or, they will provide free accommodation for key stakeholders, such as the event organiser or the client. Event organisers can also negotiate discounted room rates for event staff and crew. In addition, hotels have the ability to offer add-on facilities within the package price, such as a technical adviser, lighting engineer, sound technician, account manager, event manager, projection equipment, breakout rooms ... (or they may charge extra for these).

So, there are benefits and rewards for event organisers and clients to choose a hotel as the venue to hold their event. But, these incentives – although more available – were always there for loyal corporate clients. They do their job in winning business, but it is not enough in a rapidly changing landscape.

Hotels need to capitalise on what they offer, which alternative event venues cannot. These should include the following:

- Regulated standards in an industry that has well-established and long-standing education, apprenticeships and qualifications.
- Guaranteed professionalism drawn from personnel who are trained and experienced in the transferable skills of hospitality provision, such as customer service; catering; cleanliness; staff leadership.
- Highly regulated health and safety practices.
- Adherence to well-evolved legislation.

Events which take place in non-dedicated and unusual venues expose the client and event organiser – and the guests – to risks. There are no guarantees that management and staff at such venues are experienced, knowledgeable and qualified to the extent of those whom are employed in a hotel of good repute.

The client or event organiser cannot even be confident that dedicated venues which are built for the purpose of events offer the specialism of reputable hotels – how can a client know that a sports stadium knows how to organise a wedding?

So, hotels do hold the professional advantage here – even if it is only the perception of low risk which the client seeks. Hotels should exploit this advantage.

Hotels have a habit of rebranding and reinventing. They could rebrand their event offering, too. Instead of looking at 'The Royal Hotel' for an event, the Royal Hotel could rebrand its events offering as 'The Royal Venue', 'The Royal Events', 'The Royal for Events', 'Events at The Royal', or simply 'The Royal'. This would negate the stigma of clients resisting placing their event into a 'hotel', but would also allow The Royal to promote their events offering outside the hotel marketplace so that events organisers and clients find the hotel listed under 'venues'. If a booker has not defined their search for a 'hotel', they will not come across The Royal as a potential venue.

First, though, hotel operators need to understand how event organisers search for venues, accept that they have lost the events foothold, and identify the need to rebrand their offering.

In addition, hotels could increase the profile and awareness of what they offer as in-house services and facilities.

It is common knowledge that hotels have restaurants and kitchens – so these facilities could be marketed to the events market as 'event catering' and 'production kitchens'. The same principle could be applied to all in-situ technical apparatus – instead of 'sound and light', the language should appeal to tech managers ('faders'; 'dimmers'). This would enable production managers to recognise the capabilities of the hotel as a 'venue' and also signify that the hotel is experienced and proficient in hosting events with technical requirements.

For many years, hotels have offered a 'delegate rate' for conferences. And, conferences are synonymous with hotels. This is why the delegate rate evolved: conference organisers want to know how much it would cost for an all-inclusive package per person (*per delegate*). Hoteliers understand this demand. So, if a hotel is offering arrival coffee and pastries, room hire, technical equipment in the room, mid-morning coffee and biscuits, buffet lunch, and afternoon tea and pastries, the rate for all these inclusions would be charged per delegate.

But, hoteliers do not offer what could be called an 'event guest rate', where an event client could identify how much it would cost for an all-inclusive package *per guest*. This might include arrival drinks, canapes, room hire, production equipment in the room, dinner, a table drinks package (or amount of wine per person). Hotels could adapt and cater for this need – and pitch themselves as bona fide *event venues* to compete alongside the rival non-dedicated and unusual venues which have entered the marketplace.

Chapter 4

Venue reputation

It is important to recognise that because events have 'leaked' out of hotels and into all manner of other venues (which may be non-dedicated or unusual), and this appears to be the ongoing trend, there is greater risk of encountering a venue that is not familiar with handling events or has staff who are untrained or unqualified in the standards and procedures related to events management.

These shortfalls could be in the art of event management itself, or an incompetency in client management, the inability to meet deadlines, failing to provide resources as promised, substandard catering, non-understanding of crowd management, or lacking knowledge of health and safety requirements for events.

It is important, therefore, to establish not only whether a venue is unusual, but whether it has a team who are experienced or has the ability to host an event.

Even if a venue does have a history of hosting events, it may be that the team have evolved their version of the art. In other words, they may manage events their way, because this is the only way they know.

A specialist event organiser may easily identify the shortfalls of a venue, and should be in a position to lead the venue if that is the case. A client, however, may not realise that the splendid unusual venue of their choice is not proficient in managing events – particularly if the marketing blurb promotes themselves with a long list of hosting previous events that evokes the perception it is an 'events venue'.

Also to consider, are the additional risks associated with having to bring resources in to a non-dedicated or unusual venue. It is not unknown for suppliers to get the wrong day or deliver the wrong number of chairs. Transportation brings its own risks, too. There can be delays on roads, for example. These are not to be deemed high risks because they are infrequent, but it is risk nonetheless. Using a dedicated venue with all resources in situ, or using a hotel, negates these risks if everything is already there.

It is true that unusual venues require more resources, which not only adds risk, but means more costs and thus a higher event budget. It has already been stated how hotels can be cheaper options for events because everything is already there. So, if using a warehouse for an event, the budget must extend to resources such as additional power, lighting, kitchens, temporary toilet facilities, exterior lighting, and myriad other cost implications.

So, there are pros and cons for all types of venues. An event organiser can pick and choose according to the type of event, its location, size, number of attendees, whether overnight accommodation is required, the budget, and the complexity of the event. But, the real driver of where events are getting placed is the client. Demand dictates where the event takes place. And the demand of clients is moving towards creative, innovative events that outshines their competitors – or even outshines their own previous event.

Reputation is an unregulated industry's way of self-regulation.

What is getting better are the qualifications held by events managers now that universities offer courses in events management. The events courses themselves are a diversification from hospitality management. It could be that universities identified the diversification opportunity of a new genre of the hotel industry and designed courses to meet that opportunity. Or it may be argued that student demand led the way. The latter could be true if more people are being exposed to events such as weddings, fashion shows, concerts and festivals, where once upon a time events existed within hotels. This would follow the theory that events have evolved from hospitality and hotel management. It also supports the trend of events leaving hotels and so one does not need to be working in a hotel to come into contact with events and choose events management as a standalone and bona fide vocation.

Whatever the reasons for events management courses to now exist, it is driving the events industry towards professionalism and thus self-regulation. This is extremely helpful outside the traditional structural training of hotel managers.

It is becoming increasingly likely that any venue which hosts events will have an experienced and/or qualified events person. Or, an events specialist can be sourced by the client or the venue.

Until such time when there is full self-regulation in the industry of events management, the risk of unprofessionalism exists. For this reason, it is worthwhile to identify the reputation of a venue.

4.1 History of a venue

Possibly the easiest and most reliable identifier of the professionalism and experience of a venue is their history of hosting events. This will determine their success of attracting event business, and perhaps their ability to retain repeat business. This is a pointer to reputation, but some venues are adept at winning business and that is where the adeptness ends.

There are venues that are extremely busy with events but this alone turns them into event factories where they churn out event after event, after event. In this instance, a venue could be focusing on their sales and revenue more than the quality of the event experience they provide to event clients and event guests. Very busy wedding venues can be guilty of this practice, where they measure the success of their performance as a sales figure only.

In cases where a venue is massively busy, there can be a tendency to evolve a culture of complacency – the 'it's-another-wedding' syndrome. Here, a bride may feel that she fits in after the last bride has left and before the next bride arrives. The routine of repeat events in such venues can make the event experience lacklustre and matter-of-fact. Unfortunately, this attitude will be endemic with all staff and management at the venue.

So, a busy venue is not always testimony of the quality of events that they provide.

4.2 Testimonials

The past-client's testimonial is a good way of testing a venue's reputation. Unhappy clients do not write good reviews. A venue should be very willing to share reviews with prospect clients. So, if the venue is reticent to do so, it could suggest they do not have any.

Venue managers should encourage satisfied clients to provide a testimonial, and if the client is happy it does not take much encouragement. Some venues, however, move on to the next piece of business without thought of how the previous piece of business can act as a marketing tool for future business. It must become part of the operational procedures to ascertain client satisfaction and get it put in to writing.

4.3 Client portfolio

Looking at a venue's client portfolio can determine the level of clients they attract. A lot of business into venues is through referrals, so it can be seen if clients are referring others to use a venue. The tell-tale signs of referrals is a range of clients in the same sector, or a range of events of the same type, because people doing business spread the word and it does not take long for word to get round not to use a venue.

If one is looking to place a corporate event in to a venue, and that venue can demonstrate a range of corporate clients within their portfolio, this is a good indicator because corporate clients will be experienced in placing their events in to venues. A corporate client will avoid any risk of an event going wrong or not being enjoyed by guests, so if this venue is winning corporate event business, it can be seen as a good sign.

Venue managers should work hard to obtain business from their target markets. Becoming a reputable venue in a market sector generates more business through word of mouth, and a good venue manager will recognise this. Savvy clients already know this and will look at a venue's client portfolio to ascertain its reputation in that sector.

4.4 Online reviews

With the popularity of online reviews, feedback can be garnered from event guests as well as clients. Okay, not all reviews are accurate or fair, and one person may have a negative experience that could be against the norm or unjustified, but at a general level it is a good indicator of the reputation of a venue.

With online reviews, it may be possible to get a broader measure of the venue – not just how they manage events, but also the quality of food, friendliness of the staff, how easy is it to find the venue, what the ambience is like, and what the sleep experience is like for overnight guests.

A venue must protect its image and reputation because every client is a reviewer, these days. This hands power to the client because a venue is powerless to control online reviews, feedback and comments. It means venue managers must raise their standards and maintain them, and they must act upon any negative reviews and correct the cause of complaint. Otherwise, a string of negative reviews will become a pattern, and the pattern becomes its reputation.

4.5 By types of events

Sometimes, it is worthwhile looking for venues that have experience of hosting the type of event one is looking to place. If looking for an unusual venue for a fashion show, has that venue hosted other fashion shows? If so, it would suggest it is a good venue for fashion shows and the venue team would have experience of hosting fashion events.

However, some clients actively avoid venues that have been used for the type of event they are looking to place. A client may wish to be the first ever fashion show in that venue, and would avoid the venue if rival designers have already used it – clients do tend to avoid the risk of allowing comparisons to be made.

A venue manager would be wise not to oversell previous events via their website or brochure – it can put clients off.

4.6 Referrals by word of mouth

By far the most reliable method of determining the reputation of a venue is by word of mouth. This is where networking within the events industry carries great value because industry-savvy professionals share information about people, ideas and places.

Where a venue can be promoted favourably on its website and in its brochure, there is no control over what people say about its services. So, more valuable, perhaps, than hearing about venues with good reputation, word of mouth provides for the learning of venues with poor reputation.

Once the good reputation of a venue is being built or has been built, the venue will naturally wish to share it with potential clients. This is not only pride, but good business practice.

Business through word-of-mouth referrals is both the most effective and least expensive form of marketing.

No venue will hide its good reputation. It will only hide its poor reputation. So, if there is no reputation whatsoever, it does not look good either way.

Events is a close-knit industry and people do talk within it. Good venues will know this and are wise to the value of industry word of mouth. A professional venue will fiercely protect its reputation. This is helpful as it self-regulates industry practice – for example, it is not good practice for a venue to poach clients from a specialist events organiser, because it will soon become known that this is a venue to avoid.

4.7 View the venue – meet the team

Whatever the reputation of the venue – even if it is known to have a good reputation – a venue must always be visited by the events organiser or client. For one thing, the venue could have had recent changes, such as a change of head chef or a new manager in place.

One must not simply take another person's word on a venue. It has to be seen and felt by the person making the decision and placing the booking. For one thing, it allows the venue a chance to make their impression. This is why it can be unfair to judge a venue on somebody else's negative opinion. Maybe, that person had a bad experience which was nothing to do with the venue's quality or professionalism.

Personalities enter into the mix as well. Sometimes, one person will not get on with the team at the venue – but this is not to say it is not a good venue. Conversely, it has been known to book a great venue, only to find that personalities clash and the relationship sours.

So, in all cases, first-hand impressions are the most valid. At least the blame – if there is any – cannot be placed on to somebody else.

AUTHOR'S VOICE BOX

I tend not to recommend venues to other people.

I feel it is up to the person looking for a venue to do their own research, like I did. I'm not being selfish, but it is a risk for me to recommend a venue that has since changed its management; or the personal dynamics of the person booking the venue does not gel with its staff and the experience turns sour. I try not to recommend things that are not within my control.

So, whenever I do talk about a venue, I always make it clear that my opinion is only how I experienced the venue when I last used it.

Chapter 5

Events as a source of income

5.1 Venues with events as the primary source of income

If a building is constructed for the purpose of events (dedicated venue) it is reasonable to assume that its primary source of income will be from the business of events.

But even venues that are not dedicated (not built for the purpose of events), such as country manor houses, castles, and those premises which have changed their use, such as a former fire station or former brewery, for example, may now consider events to be their main revenue stream and the primary source of income.

Any venue which is now considering events to be their sole or primary income stream must have the facilities, manpower and expertise in-house to meet client and guest expectations and needs. The volume of events will be at a level which generates the primary income, so it follows that the venue will be well equipped and staffed to manage events.

It could be that a venue does not host high volumes of events, but nevertheless is receiving primary revenue from events. In such cases, the venue manager will outsource the event expertise to event organisers or event management companies. Indeed, some venue owners may go so far as to unlock the doors and switch on the lights for viewings, but would have no expertise in the management of events and would rely on the client to be serviced by an event organiser or event management company.

So, it does not follow that a venue with events as their primary source of income is always a place which is competent in event management, client management, and guest management.

It must be remembered that a musician or band's success is often measured by their ability to sell-out stadium tours, which is a major step up from arena tours. In such instances, the sports stadium becomes a concert venue. But, the art of managing sports events is not the same art as managing a concert.

In addition, it does not follow that because a purpose-built venue is called a conference centre, its sole ability is to host conferences. Most venues are flexible with their facilities and spaces so that they can diversify to host a range of types of events, thus widening their reach to a broader spectrum of events business.

A common issue with venues diversifying their range of events is that the infrastructure may be suitable for one type of event but not another. Kitchens, for example could be sited at one side of the venue making it difficult for a banquet to be served. This is the case at London's O2 arena and it makes it logistically very difficult for servicing their large-scale dining events such as the BRIT Awards.

The infrastructure of a venue may be good to go, and the management and staff may have abilities in security, venue management, staffing and crowd management. But, there are differences between opening a sports stadium for a football match and opening it for a rock concert. This is where the venue would dovetail their strengths with the strengths of a professional team in the type of event being placed into the venue.

Venue managers must be cautious when receiving enquiries from events outside their usual remit, even if their venue can accommodate the booking. Overstretching a field of expertise into another field, such as another type of event, can convert venue strengths into their weaknesses.

Whatever the type of venue, and whatever the range of events it can accommodate, if it is a dedicated venue its primary source of income will be derived from events. But, the booker must understand where lies the field of expertise, nonetheless.

5.2 Venues with events as their secondary source of income

Not all venues consider events to be their core business.

Many premises of all types, uses and sizes have realised the potential to generate additional income through events. These would include lofts, unused buildings, disused warehouses, wharfs, manufacturing sites, car showrooms, office headquarters, banks, government offices, art galleries, museums, shopping centres, parklands and open spaces, and any buildings considered to be of architectural interest.

> ### AUTHOR'S VOICE BOX
>
> Thorpe Park in Surrey is a water-based theme park constructed around partially flooded gravel pits. It is a successful format which attracts 1.8 million visitors each year.
>
> When I joined the company, events were viewed as a side attraction to facilitate the odd request for a company barbecue or a corporate fun day on the rides.
>
> As a young and eager employee, I realised the potential for achieving revenue from events and I grew the events from a splinter-section of another department into a standalone department that was positioned to market itself to the events industry and meet the needs of corporate clients.
>
> When the park's directors saw an increase in contribution from events to the core business of the park's rides, I was supported in providing more private spaces to accommodate larger numbers and more clients for a wider range of events from boat shows to craft fairs.
>
> Here was a landmark location with excellent facilities to attract corporate clients, and a readymade infrastructure to support dining, partying, entertainment and even parking for attendees at large events.
>
> One of my clients wanted to rent the park for three evenings after it had closed to the general public. This required installation of lights for the first time in the park's history. The success of these evenings and the fact that the lighting was in place led to 'dark hours opening' and eventually to the successful 'Fright Nights' concept.
>
> Additionally, my department operated over the winter months when the park was closed to the public. This achieved revenue from exhibitions, conferences, dinners, meetings and Christmas parties. Events was the only contributor of revenue during the park's closed season when the income would otherwise have been zero.
>
> This demonstrates the impact events can have on the revenue of a business where events are not the core revenue provider.

AUTHOR'S VOICE BOX

When I was on the management team of the inaugural Party in the Park event in 1998 for Prince Charles's The Princes Trust, it was unheard of for permission to be granted for a closed event in Hyde Park – a designated royal park.

One may argue that the Party in the Park open-air concert was an event for the public. But, the public needed to purchase tickets for admission, so it was not in the true spirit of an open royal park with a royal charter to be accessible to all.

The amazing success of the event, the profile it raised for His Royal Highness's charity and the funds it contributed to both the charity and the Royal Parks Department, enabled the event to reoccur the following year and each subsequent year, leading to the established Route of Kings annual concerts.

This was proof that events contribute significant additional income outside the core purpose of the venue – and it was proof with a royal seal of approval.

All manner of buildings and premises have learnt how to generate secondary income from events. Nowadays, almost every commercial building in London – large and small – will consider hosting events, even if they have never done so before.

Highclere Castle in Berkshire, UK, provides an example of a non-dedicated event venue that has achieved immense success from events, so that events contribute significant income to the core business.

Highclere is a stately home and working farm. For many years, its main source of income was from ticket sales as a country house attraction with visitors paying for access to the magnificent home and fine grounds. It also hosted small and medium sized events, such as weddings, conferences and an annual jazz festival.

I was once invited to Highclere Castle to provide ideas and advice on how to generate income from events and grow their existing portfolio.

A short while afterwards, a television production company negotiated the use of Highclere as a set for filming a drama series called *Downton Abbey*.

Now, Highclere Castle attracts more visitors than ever before!

28 THE MANAGEMENT OF EVENT VENUES

Events extend the contribution of income for non-event venues.

In the case of the Natural History Museum in London, the building has become as renowned for its events, as it is for its fine museum exhibits. Indeed, for many years London Fashion Week was held under marquees on the museum's lawn. Events also occur in the Victoria & Albert Museum, the Science Museum, the British Museum and every museum in the land, because museums struggle with generating income and so they have diversified to become event venues.

Because events are now seen to reap additional income, they are happening in premises that were previously inaccessible, such as governmental buildings, private clubs, disused Underground stations, and premises of the Royal Palaces. Even the law courts – the Royal Courts of Justice – can be booked for private events.

Madame Tussauds is widely known as a successful events venue. Yet, even here the events are secondary to the core business of exhibiting waxworks of celebrities and notable figures in society. When the daytime paying visitors leave, Madame Tussauds generates secondary income from hosting dinners, presentations and other celebrations in their galleries, with iconic figures from music, history and royalty looking over the shoulders of event guests as they dine.

Chapter 6

Venue professionalism

The drawback to the growth and diversity of event venues is that clients and their guests are more at risk of being exposed to venues which are unprofessional or inexperienced at managing events.

In the traditional environment of events being staged in hotels and purpose-built dedicated venues, such as conference centres, the client may have justly felt that their event would be in safe hands. After all, most reputable hotels are experienced in the organisation of events. And, if a client were to book a conference centre for their conference, it would be reasonable to assume that the venue would be experienced in running a conference.

Certainly, dedicated venues seek to employ staff for the very business of events. These staff will be recruited for their experience, knowledge and qualifications – it would make sense to do so, and the labour expense would be justified. Whereas, the staff at a venue such as a museum, may not be as proficient (nor interested) in the good management of events.

Sure, there are no guarantees that even a 'traditional' event venue will, in fact, be proficient in organising events – as with 'bad' hotels and 'bad' restaurants, 'bad' venues do exist – let's call them 'wrong' from here onwards.

The difference between a good and 'wrong' hotel, restaurant or venue is a matter of the training and experience of the management and staff.

Training and experience determines *professionalism*.

Hotels, restaurants and venues form the *hospitality service industry* and it is largely self-regulated or unregulated. Yes, it is regulated by legislation such as food hygiene, health and safety, licensing laws, and employment regulations, but one does not require a qualification to be a hotelier or restaurateur – this is where the 'wrong' creeps in to the industry. Many hotels are wrongly run (either from a business perspective or a customer experience perspective) because the owner or manager is unqualified and inexperienced. Of course this differs from regulated sectors of society such as education or medicine.

Events management is only an offshoot of hospitality management and in events there is no experience or qualification necessary to set up shop and perform the operation.

It used to be that the 'events industry' was indefinable – tacked on to the hotel and catering industry, because events happened in hotels.

People did not choose a career in events management, but fell into it by accident because they happened to be working in the conference and banqueting department of a hotel. Or, they had to organise a company occasion, like a conference or the office Christmas party, and this is how they became an 'event manager'. Certainly, no events management courses existed and nobody really knew what 'event management' was about.

Lack of training in events management, plus inexperience of organising and running events, is still the problem. But, all the time there is better and more available training for people working in events. Events management has evolved in to a bona fide and recognised career choice.

Events management has matured into a standalone career path.

Other than good training for management and staff, and their experience of organising quality events, the rise of internet reviews does keep hotels, restaurants and event venues in check. This is a good thing: it is self-regulation. It will not be long before clients begin asking to see the qualifications of the staff in whom they entrust the management of their event. Already, clients are looking at how experienced is the venue and its staff.

Wrong venues are not the norm anymore, which is possibly why they are more visible and easier to avoid. It is no longer so easy for a wrongly run venue to exist or sustain itself in the evolving industry of events.

Also, everybody's expectations of events are higher than ever before. Event clients have increasingly higher demands not only for the creativity of the content of their event, but for the service levels delivered by the venue. It is the clients who continue to extend the boundaries and drive the demand for better technology, standards and creativity.

Guests have higher expectations, as well. They are attending ever-more-sophisticated events and expect their next event experience to exceed the previous. For a guest, every event they attend is a learning curve which serves to educate them as to what is achievable. This is visible in the rise of 'experiential' events which aim to deliver to the senses of those attending.

The question is what determines a good venue from a wrong venue? And, because there is a vast spectrum of wrongness, how to identify just how wrong a venue is?

Well, it is widely known what makes a good restaurant. Yes; it is the food.

And, it is known that good cooking requires a trained an experienced chef. But, a restaurant customer's satisfaction does not stop at what is served on the plate. A good restaurant is also determined and measured by its ambience, service, comfort and friendliness. In short, it is 'the meal experience' – the entire experience a customer receives from the moment they walk into the restaurant, to the moment they exit. Everything they experience between arrival and departure is the 'meal experience'.

This philosophy can be attributed to event venues – we may call it 'the guest experience'. This is everything the event guest (or the event client for that matter) experiences from the moment they arrive at the venue to the moment they leave. Everything experienced between – the welcome; friendliness; service; cleanliness; attention to detail; attention to safety; proficiency of technical staff; the ambience; the look and feel; and the *professionalism* of the entire team – all these, separately and together, determine 'the guest experience'.

So, how does an event venue achieve a good guest experience? And, how can the event guest or event client know whether the experience is going to be good or wrong?

It should be noted here that it is not only the reputation of a venue which is at stake with an event. The client's reputation is exposed, too. Always, the client will be inviting guests, so their own choices and professionalism are on display. It can be extremely embarrassing – not to mention damaging – for a client to get a wrong venue. If it is a corporate client, their professional reputation – and even their job – could be at stake.

The problem here is the time factor.

With a restaurant the judgement of whether it is good or wrong can be instant. This is only because people know what indicators to look for. It comes upon entering the restaurant – the beginning of the 'meal experience', remember – the cleanliness; friendliness; quick and efficient service. Then, the food is eaten and judged.

With a hotel it is also a quick judgement. Again, it is cleanliness, friendliness and efficiency of service that is under scrutiny from the outset.

However, with an event the results are not instant. The preparations (the *lead-in*) to the event can be three months or even much longer, during which time it is too late to judge the venue because it was booked, confirmed and a deposit paid at the outset. Loss of the deposit aside, it is also difficult to change a venue once a decision has been made because the location would have been notified to attendees, suppliers, and other stakeholders. Often, it is the result of the event itself – the day of the event – which determines the right or wrongness of a venue, by which time the event is already happening.

But, just as with restaurants and hotels, the tell-tale signs of a good or wrong venue are there at the beginning.

If the client or booker thinks about what determines a good restaurant from the outset it will transfer to event venues as well: reputation; look and feel; cleanliness; approach of the staff; a demonstration (or feeling) of professionalism; their experience; reviews…

Thus, when choosing a venue for an event, the judgement of whether it is a good or wrong venue can be instant.

Where these indicators are not visible – hotels and restaurants can be booked in advance (over the phone, for example) and so will an event venue – then it comes down to reputation: word of mouth or online review sites before taking the plunge to go ahead and book. Here the event venue has an advantage over hotels and restaurants, because unlike walking into a restaurant or checking into a hotel, an event client will not book a venue without first having visited it. This safeguards the client (if they know what indicators to look for) and provides the opportunity for venue managers to ensure the pre-event visit (the *venue show-round*) goes extremely well.

So, a venue show-round is not just a marketing opportunity for the venue to sell themselves to a client. Nor is it solely for the client to check out a venue. It is a two-way mirror to reveal the fit and spot the wrinkles.

All the effort of an event venue manager amounts to one word: reputation.

> **AUTHOR'S VOICE BOX**
>
> At one venue I recently visited, I noticed how the large potted palms under the glass roof in the courtyard were in very poor condition: they were thirsty, dusty and uncared-for.
>
> I was considering to recommend this venue to my client in which they may entertain their guests. So, I would rather have seen healthy and well-maintained plants. Or, I would prefer there were no plants whatsoever, rather than a scattering of poorly kept specimens.
>
> This alone was not a serious issue. After all, I could remove the palms before the event began. I could replace them with healthy green plants, if I so desired.
>
> But, seeing the uncared-for plants did serve to forewarn me that a problem with good management existed at that venue – at the very least it was poor housekeeping.
>
> The point is not to avoid an unprofessional venue, but to identify it.
>
> If I have identified that a venue is not professional, as in this case, I can manage those inadequacies. Not always will I walk away.
>
> It does mean I may have limited support from the venue – I might have to provide a cleaning crew under my control, for example. Even if the venue is friendly and willing, it is helpful to identify their shortfalls from the outset.
>
> Often, all I need is the four walls and a roof over our head, and the rest I will outsource from my own trusted and reliable providers if I have to.

Once the indicators are known, the distinction between a good and a wrong venue becomes easier to identify.

Long before any guests arrive, the event client (which could be a private client, corporate client, or a specialist event organiser) will arrive to the venue to consider booking it for the event – this will happen at the earliest stage of the planning period (the *lead-in*).

If the client is an event specialist and not the final decision maker, they will certainly be recommending the venue to their client. So, whoever is the client, if the

34 THE MANAGEMENT OF EVENT VENUES

venue should turn out to be wrong it is a serious negative reflection upon their judgement and experience.

Here, it can be seen that another reputation can be added to the list – not only the venue's reputation for hosting events, and that of the client for booking the venue, but also the reputation of the event specialist for recommending the venue.

6.1 What makes a 'good' venue

The first identification of a 'good' venue is in the detail. *How well is it run?*

Ascertaining whether a venue is run well is not down to one element, but many factors which contribute to the whole and provide the experienced eye with a full-on wink of approval or disapproval.

6.1.1 Cleanliness

How clean a venue appears is always a good first indicator. Good cleaning is not a luxury, but a basic expectation. As has been already identified, an unclean hotel room or a dirty restaurant is easy to recognise as unacceptable. It is the same principle with an event venue, once cleanliness is recognised as being a key indicator.

An unclean venue is not only indicative of bad management in allowing clients and guests to have an event in a dirty or unhygienic environment, but is bad behaviour, too.

If a venue cannot manage an effective cleaning regime, it is a reflection of their poor and ineffective standards of management throughout.

Venue managers must not underestimate the importance of good housekeeping. Every client or potential booker has the ability to identify clean from dirty. The easy part is that there is no in-between measure: if it is not clean, it is dirty.

Displaying poor housekeeping means that the venue manager does not care; or is not interested in details; or is lacking pride, energy, effort or commitment. Whichever it is, is not important because the first indicator (poor cleaning) signals the problem, not the symptoms.

A good client will not stick around long enough to understand why a venue is dirty, and may not even indicate this is why they are rejecting the venue. Clients tend not to offend and will decline politely. Besides, if a client is not going to book the venue, why should they bother to describe the reason? So, a venue manager may not know why potential clients are choosing competitor venues.

The glaring issue with poor housekeeping is that the causes will carry throughout the management of the venue. If a venue manager is not taking care of details, this will be the same with all other details. If it is down to poor leadership, the staffing team at the venue will likely also be poorly led in the kitchen, the bar, reception, and most everywhere else. This is why cleanliness is such an important and obvious first indicator.

6.1.2 Appearance

If a venue appears tired and tatty, then so may its attitude towards event clients. If the management are struggling with the upkeep of the venue, it suggests either a lack of interest or a lack of the level of business. The management's priority may be purely financial gain or financial austerity – they are not reinvesting in their offering, which could affect the quality of service and the support they provide to event clients.

6.1.3 Enquiry handling

Often, the way a venue handles an enquiry sets the precedent for further communication and approach procedures.

Enquiries are the first client-to-venue contact. If the enquiry handling procedure is unprofessional, unhelpful or unwilling, it suggests this is the way the management process will follow at that venue.

6.1.4 Response

After the enquiry, a good indicator of a venue's strengths and weaknesses will be in their response to the enquiry or subsequent questions that the client needs satisfied.

Responses can be measured by the venue's willingness to provide answers, how long it takes to respond and whether their experience of events enables them to adequately answer the client's questions.

6.1.5 Procedures

It usually becomes apparent early on whether a venue has effective procedures for handling enquiries, bookings, show-rounds and confirmations. If any part of this procedural process gets passed around the management team, it suggests an ineffective management structure exists (see 9.0 for a detailed explanation of the venue management structure).

Each of the indicators stated above enables the client or organiser to 'instantly' judge an event venue, just as if they were checking into a hotel or being seated at a table in a restaurant. It is important, therefore, for the venue manager to view each indicator and measure how a prospective client would view their venue.

A venue manager must understand the factors by which clients reach the decision to book or reject a venue for their event. However, it is not enough to know them – most venue managers would know the factors if they were asked – so it is important to recognise them and measure them from the perspective of a client visiting their venue for the first time.

A professional venue will have made sure to build its good reputation. It is the mainstay of a venue's business to do so.

Referring again to London's Natural History Museum as an example, it is a hugely successful venue with sustainable events business due largely by maintaining its reputation as a magnificent venue to hold events.

When a client or event organiser books a venue, they want to feel assured that their event is being held at a reputable and experienced venue, just by the volume of business it satisfies. Peace of mind: what more could a client ask when choosing a venue for their event?

There are three tools to *avoid* when ascertaining a venue's reputation.

1. It is not a good idea to garner opinions from local competitors. Opinions from competing venues cannot be taken as genuine or unbiased.

2. Do not rely on the venue's own marketing (website or brochure). A good web designer or graphic designer will make the venue look attractive – it does not mean the venue knows how to organise events.

    In addition, the client list on a venue's website or in their brochure could be historic – perhaps under previous ownership or management. Venues last longer than people.

3. The venue's staff, management and sales personnel may not lie about the professionalism and experience of the venue at which they are employed, but their opinions certainly cannot be taken as unbiased.

VENUE PROFESSIONALISM

> **AUTHOR'S VOICE BOX**
>
> When I was the head of events at a well-known central London venue, potential clients would visit for a show-round and did often ask about my nearest competitor.
>
> This was never awkward for me. After all, I knew my competitor existed along the road and it was fair and right for clients who were searching for somewhere to hold their event, to visit other venues in the vicinity. So, I never would provide negative comments. I would simply suggest that they visit my competitor themselves and make up their own mind. Besides, I was very aware of my competitor's weaknesses and I was confident that if a client visited them, they would sniff them out.
>
> This nearest competitor, however, would always give potential clients a negative opinion about my venue.
>
> I don't know how many clients (if any) were put off my venue by my competitor's underhand tactic. But, I do know how many clients told me they considered my competitor to be unprofessional because of how they derided my venue. I feel confident the latter is far greater than the former.

It must be remembered that the venue must satisfy the event organiser, the client *and* the guests. It can be identified, then, that there are four distinct parties involved with any event:

1. The venue event manager – the person running the venue, or running the event on behalf of the venue.

2. The event organiser – this person may be the client, or could be an events specialist or events company hired by the client.

3. The client – the person paying the bill for the event.

    This person could be a private client, such as for a wedding, birthday party or anniversary party; or a direct client, such as a club promoter or quiz organiser, or a corporate client on behalf of an organisation.

    A venue should note that the client may also be the event organiser, such as an event specialist or agency hired to manage the event, or may *not* be the organiser and would either expect the venue to organise the event, or would engage the services of a specialist event organiser or agency.

4. The guest who attends the event.

In addition to these four interested parties, there are other stakeholders who would have an interest in the choice and capability of the venue:

5   Sponsors – think of where their product will be exposed.
6   Press – think of camera angles, press rooms, interview rooms, ease of access to the location.
7   Caterers and other service providers, such as furniture hire companies and decorators – think of the style of venue, its location, access and delivery points.
8   Entertainers, such as bands, speakers, presenters.
9   Technical, such as crew and management – think of the acoustics, ceiling height, visibility.
10 Security – think of VIP areas, exits that require security, car drop-off points.
11 Legal, licensing and permission providers, such as police, medics, fire, local authorities, risk assessors, environmental health.
12 Local residents who may be affected by volume of visitors, increased traffic, noise disturbance.

6.2 Venue show-round

A venue show-round (or venue *recce* – short for reconnaissance) is where a client or event organiser visits a potential venue for their event and receives a show-round of the facilities and spaces by the event manager or venue manager.

It is extremely rare for a booking to confirm without the client first viewing the venue. Of course, if the client has used the venue before, the booking may go ahead without a show-round.

Event organisers and event companies will bring their client to view venues they have identified as being suitable for the event. This could be just one venue – the best they have identified as a fit for the event – or it could be two or three venues to view and the organiser will make the decision with the client after viewing these venues.

Often, organisers will visit venues in advance of bringing a client to view. This is the preferred way because the organiser can liaise with the venue, negotiate rates, get the logistics planned, and establish a relationship with the venue manager before the client is present. In such cases the organiser's show-round can be made in advance of the client's visit, or it could take place on the same day but before the client arrives.

Viewing in advance of the client also allows the organiser to plan their route to the venue and make sure they know how to gain access and who to deal with. It is professional to have visited the venue in advance and demonstrate to the client that the organiser is familiar with the venue manager.

Some organisers, however, will visit a venue for the first time with their client. This can be because of limitations with time or the location, or where the organiser has a familiar relationship with their client and can be open with the venue in front of the client.

From the venue's point of view, a venue show-round is an event and should be treated as such.

This means the approach to show-rounds requires procedures, preparation and planning.

A venue manager should first understand the indicator factors identified in section 6.1 of this book and how they influence the decisions of potential clients viewing the venue.

It is also imperative to present the venue in a professional manager and have procedures in place to do so. These would include the following.

- Ensuring the venue is clean from previous events or other activities.
- Ensuring the venue is accessible and that no other events are taking place where areas and spaces are not available to view.
- Ensuring the entire staff are aware of a client being in the venue for a show-round.
- Setting the venue in the correct mode for the type of enquiry. So, if the client is viewing for a fashion show, the venue should be set for a show; if the event is to be a party, the venue should be set for a party. This may include sound, lighting, projection, furniture layout.
- Providing hospitality such as coffee on arrival, chilled water, lunch.
- Providing a quiet place to discuss the event.

Venues exist in a competitive marketplace and with more event clients seeking unusual and creative venues, the competition is ever-increasing. It is usual for a client to identify two or three venues or locations and visit each before making a decision to book.

The show-round is the venue's sales opportunity and a chance to promote its professionalism. This is difficult to achieve if the show-round does not go well. To ensure it does go well requires planning to lessen any risk of a show-round failing.

The show-round not only provides a first impression, it may provide the only impression.

So, a venue manager must take each show-round event seriously and not treat it merely as a 'prospect' or a 'chance' of a booking. In fact, a show-round is the opportunity to secure the booking. After all, if the client or organiser has scheduled a show-round, they have already identified the venue as being suitable for their event.

Clients will quickly identify a laisse-faire attitude as easily as they can identify if the venue is clean or dirty: it is easy to spot. This will drive them to choose a competitor venue.

Also, clients will be driven away by a clear 'salesy' venue manager who will promise everything just to get the booking. Clients like to make their choice and not be pushed into it by sales patter. Remember; the show-round is an opportunity to demonstrate professionalism, not 'sell' the venue.

Mostly, clients appreciate honesty. It is not honest for a venue manager to run down a competitor's venue. And, if the venue is not a fit for one reason or another, the venue manager should be honest and let the booking go elsewhere. It is a too common mistake for a venue to grab whatever business comes its way and not be able to execute a successful event. It is better to have no booking than a wrong booking.

Chapter 7

The need to meet expectations

It should be kept in mind that there are four distinct parties involved with venues and events.

1 The venue event manager (employed by the venue).
2 The event organiser (specialist event organiser or event company).
3 The client (who may or may not be the event organiser).
4 The guest who attends the event.

The exodus from traditional venues has fuelled the need for event organisers to impress their guests. Event creativity, decoration, entertainment and the entire 'guest experience' (what is now termed as *experiential events*) each play their important role in satisfying or exceeding guests' expectations – or failing them.

The *venue* is a key element of reaching guests' expectations at an event.

An exciting environment is the linchpin of whether the event will be successful. It has not always been this way. At one time, event organisers would have chosen a venue for its functionality and practicality. If the venue was in a good enough location and could accommodate the basic requirements of the event, it would be chosen. Once, that was all it took to satisfy the client and the guests.

Nowadays, functionality and practicality do not reach far enough. Clients want something more. Their guests expect it. This demands that the venue must meet or surpass all expectations.

The evolvement of the events industry has taken events business out of hotels and into the cold harsh world of 'unsafe' venues where professionalism and expertise is not assured.

Anybody in the position of booking a venue can no longer leave it to chance and hope that they can rely on the venue to make everything go smoothly.

Anybody in the position of recommending venues to clients – normally specialist event organisers – has their reputation and future business to consider and must therefore be able to distinguish good venues from wrong venues. Most organisers build a portfolio of known and trusted venues.

Anybody in the position of visiting a venue as a guest should at least possess an understanding of what to expect from the venue and what to do if their expectations are not met.

Venues themselves are in the position to meet the expectations of all those mentioned above.

If the above parties were to pool their knowledge – the venue managers, venue bookers, event clients, event organisers and event guests – then the evolvement of the events industry would be successful for everybody in it... which *is* everybody.

Venue managers must keep up with the changing demands and expectations of their private clients, corporate clients, their specialist event-organiser clients, and the guests who attend their venue. Otherwise, their venue will fall behind their competitors.

The explosion of events into non-traditional venues provides opportunity for all sorts of premises, companies and private landowners to earn income from hiring out their facilities for events. This is why more people need to be provided with the skills to meet the demands and expectations of event clients and their guests.

AUTHOR'S VOICE BOX

Paris Hilton, who is worth an estimated $100 million, has realised the exciting potential of earning a little extra income from events. She rented out her $5.9m home in Beverly Hills as a venue for the filming of The Bling Ring.

Source: Daily Mail, 13 June 2013

Chapter 8

Venue culture change

There are venues which are obliged to host events even if they do not really wish to. It is as if they are forced into hosting events simply because there is a demand for them to do so.

Demand could be a one-off enquiry for using the premises for an event, or it could be repetitive because the venue has some attraction, such as interesting architecture or is at a prominent location. Such venues – and their staff – can consider events as an interruption to the core business.

For example, a museum with interesting architecture might be hosting an evening canapé reception and the museum staff may feel inconvenienced that they must stay late to work at the event. Door staff will be required to stay longer; the cloakroom must be manned until the last guest leaves; cleaning staff face an additional workload on the morning after the event... Everybody's day is lengthened and their daily work routine is interrupted. For staff who have a usual work pattern, it is most disruptive to stay late at work – they may have to make arrangements for their children to be met from school; or they will miss their usual bus or train home from work; they will arrive home late, so their evening routine is disrupted. Staff do not always welcome changes to their routine workday.

Sure, overtime payments are always welcome, but this may not be perceived as worth the late hours and out-of-hours inconvenience.

An employee's resentment at having to work an event is understandable – especially if, as a museum employee, say, they did not choose events as a career option.

Unfortunately, any negative elements will reflect poorly on the result: the event.

It is essential, therefore, for any venue which finds itself in the position of hosting an event, to do so professionally and ensure the staff are carried along with the idea.

Doing it right is not a choice.

As any business adviser will confirm, resistance to change is due to poor communication.

If the management approach is right, staff at the museum will be shown to realise how an event can contribute significantly to the success of the organisation which employs them. This means secure jobs.

But, staff will not always recognise this unless it is communicated to them or they see the impact on their wage slip. Even then, what arrives in their pay packet must be worthwhile for the inconvenience of working at the event or taking on an additional workload because of it.

It is important that staff who are carrying the success of the event and the success of the business are included in a share of these successes.

Staff are the frontline of any venue and can make the event special for both the client and the guests. Understanding this basic correlation is crucial if a venue is going to win business, retain business, and build and maintain its good reputation.

8.1 The need for good communication

The key to good venue management is good interdepartmental communication.

The situation which most often arises at non-dedicated venues is that the staff simply do not understand the business of events. To them, an impending event is the cause of inconvenience and disruption, as outlined above.

A barman, cleaner or security attendant may be adept at their job, but they may not appreciate the complexities of organising an event, meeting corporate expectations and satisfying a client.

Staff may not understand that the needs and expectations of a corporate client and their guests are going to be different to satisfying the person who normally patronises the core business – a library visitor, perhaps.

Crucially, the staff may not even care about these differences, let alone identify them or begin to try to understand them.

Helping staff to care about events is the role of the venue manager, even if the venue is not an event venue, but a library.

Culture change within the organisation is necessary – and it is very possible to achieve.

> **AUTHOR'S VOICE BOX**
>
> In my role as the head of events at various non-dedicated venues, I have consistently proved that as the culture shifts within the organisation or venue, staff will actively seek to participate with events.
>
> At one venue where staff members resented events because of the change to their daily work pattern, their participation in successful events soon resulted in them looking forward to the next event that would insert variety into their otherwise mundane work routine.
>
> Quite quickly, I was getting hounded by staff who wanted the next event to happen. In turn, this put pressure on me to increase the level of events. What an excellent sales incentive *that* was!

The primary objective is inclusion.

When staff become included in the process of organising an event, they will begin to feel responsible for their part in making that event a success. Inclusion begins with communication.

The suggestion here is not to include staff with the *management* of the event, but in the communication procedures of the event. In other words, they have their job to do, but they can do it within the context of understanding the event manager's role.

46 THE MANAGEMENT OF EVENT VENUES

8.1.1 Here is a case study example – the zoo

The staff at the zoo do not respond well to a corporate client wanting to have a buffet lunch served out in the garden by the waterfall, whereas all other zoo visitors are happy to eat in the restaurants or designated picnic areas. The inconveniences of this request are that the garden has to be closed to the public, tables and chairs need to be set up in the garden, the restaurant staff have to serve food out there in addition to serving zoo visitors in the restaurant, the garden has to be cleared after the corporate clients have eaten, and finally the area will require cleaning before it can be reopened to the public. For the zoo staff whom have to do all this, the logistics of this request may not seem worth the effort.

But, if the zoo venue manager were to communicate that the event is worth £12,000 income, that the client is entertaining international investors to the city where the zoo is located, that the client wants a private area for their guests and they like the view from where the fountain garden is, that there is real potential for ongoing repeat bookings from this client, that the client had been looking at an alternative venue but decided to book our zoo... If all this valuable information gets communicated to the staff, they would not have a problem with the minor inconveniences of a lunch served by the fountain in the garden.

Indeed, the staff may enjoy the experience of serving food by the fountain in the sunshine for a change, rather than in the restaurant as they do every other day.

It can be that the zoo staff will be asking if they can do this again, and when is the next booking like this going to happen.

If dining in the garden becomes a regular request, staff will adapt to the need and will miss it when it does not happen. And, it all happened because the staff understood who the client is, what they want, why they want it, and its value to the business that pays their wages.

Variances in routine can identify new working practices, so they should at least be investigated. If, in the zoo example, the ambience and logistics of serving lunch in the fountain garden proved successful, it may be that this would become a venue for group lunches for zoo visitors as well as event guests.

8.2 Interdepartmental communication

Where there are departmental divisions at a venue, effective interdepartmental communication is the *only* way the venue can operate good events.

The word 'only' is used with purpose. Events are a team effort because they require many elements to be drawn together to achieve the goal of success. These elements must be provided by a range of staff and specialists, without whom the event will not work.

Considering that the venue is the key element to the success of an event and that elements for the event will be drawn from various departments – kitchen, bar, reception, bedrooms – clearly, the events department cannot facilitate the event alone.

Therefore, it is impossible for an event to succeed if the departments are not working together. And, the *only* way of working together is through effective communication.

Venues and hotels are departmental environments. The nature of departmentalisation means that departments tend to work autonomously within their own parameters. The staff can develop their own micro-environment and in some cases they do not interact with other departments within the same venue or organisation. This is a frequent factor in hotels where one department fails to interrelate with another.

Much research and writing has been done on this subject and educated hoteliers know to encourage cross-departmental relations.

Informal communication and team-work techniques such as staff social events are implemented not just for fun, but to get departments interacting with each other. 'Nudging' staff members to interact through social activities helps people get along. They begin to understand each other, appreciate their individualism and identify like-minded colleagues outside the physical barriers of working within departments.

Structured methods of communication need to be introduced, too. These can include daily operations meetings for all departments to discuss business of the current day; heads of department meetings to share department information with other departments; and events meetings to specifically communicate details of forthcoming events to the departments which will be affected. Often, the heads of department meeting will allow for discussing forthcoming events.

8.2.1 Event forecast (example in Appendix I)

The event forecast is a list of forthcoming events.

It will contain less detail than a function sheet (see 8.2.2) as its purpose is to provide basic information to other departments which need advance warning to arrange logistics such as staffing levels, or ordering items such as food products which may have lag times due to ordering and delivery processes.

Typically, an event forecast will show information such as the date of the event, its location in the venue such as which room(s), other requirements such as bedrooms, the type of event, and the number of guests attending.

Depending on the venue, an event forecast can show forthcoming events for a ten day period, fortnightly period or monthly period.

8.2.2 Function sheet (see Appendix III)

The function sheet is a detailed information document and is produced for each event. It provides an activity timeline for the lead-in to the event, the day of the event, and any activities required to carry out post-event.

A function sheet is built organically during the preparation period (*lead-in*) of the event. As details and logistics become known, so they are added to the function sheet and this document takes shape. Building it this way avoids forgetting to include something that should be on the function sheet, and it helps to see how the event is taking shape as elements get drawn together and set in place on the running order.

The running order forms part of the function sheet and is a list of activities that are due to take place, when they should take place, and who is responsible for them taking place.

At some point close to the date of the event, everything will be in place and so there is nothing more to add and the function sheet is complete. At this point, the function sheet can be distributed to key stakeholders (see below). The completion point will vary from event to event due to variations in event size, nature and complexity, but it will be close enough to the event so that there are no changes to the schedule, yet with time to allow for key stakeholders to review it and raise any issues.

Where a function sheet has been distributed and there are changes to be made because some element of the event has changed or is now included at a late stage, or because a key stakeholder has identified an issue, a second edition will be published and distributed. Some venues prefer to issue a 'draft' function sheet for these reasons and will thereafter distribute the 'final' function sheet.

The function sheet becomes the guide sheet for all parties working the event. Every detail is contained within this document and nothing must happen at the event if it is not on the function sheet.

List of key stakeholders for distributing the function sheet:

VENUE CULTURE CHANGE

- Event organiser/venue manager.
- Technical or production manager.
- All departments at the venue – usually distributed to the head of each department.
- Client (running order only).
- Caterer or kitchen.
- Suppliers (running order only).
- Sponsors (running order only).

On the day of the event, the function sheet is used to brief the staff and copies of the running order only can be placed in departments such as the bar and the kitchen for staff to refer if they have any doubts or receive queries from guests.

8.2.3 Briefing meetings

The event organiser will brief members of the team at various key stages. The first stage will be at a departmental level – the heads of department meeting. This would outline the forthcoming event, and information may be limited so could be taken from the event forecast (see 8.2.1).

The next opportunity to brief other parties would be at the operations meeting on the day of the event.

After this, there would be an event briefing for staff working the event. This briefing meeting would be scheduled on to the function sheet (see 8.2.2) to take place 30 minutes before the doors open to guests. This close timing allows for most of the set-up to have taken place and staff should be free to attend a ten-minute briefing. Nothing is going to change at this late stage. After the briefing meeting, staff can return to complete final touches to their area before the doors open and guests enter the venue.

Where there is opportunity to do so, a pre-event briefing can be scheduled. This would take place before the day of the event. Pre-event briefings are usually for key members of the event team who will be busy and unavailable to attend the staff briefing on the event day. Besides, the staff briefing is for operational details, whereas a pre-event briefing is at managerial level.

Also, it would be impractical to call staff in for a briefing before the day of the event because some staff will be working just for the event – bar and waiting staff, for example. It would cost to bring staff in for a pre-event briefing, so this is why the staff briefing happens on the day.

Sometimes, however, it is necessary to bring staff in for a pre-event briefing – if it is a large event with a lot of staff and it would not be viable to brief them all on the day of the event. This is often the case with challenge events, such as running events and bike ride events, where large numbers of volunteers are used to marshal the route. Logistically, it would be better to call all staff in for an hour's briefing before the day of the event.

Of course, there would be no cost for requiring volunteers to attend a pre-event briefing.

In the 'zoo garden' case study example, it is easy to identify what the event organiser needs to communicate to the staff.

Value of the event

Informing the staff that the event was worth £12,000 income would demonstrate the importance of this client to the company and how much the client has outlaid for the experience of having lunch served at the fountain in the garden. This also makes the effort worthwhile.

In the zoo example, where core business zoo visitors pay individual ticket prices, the value of a corporate booking will seem very impressive to the staff.

The client

If the zoo staff are made aware of who the client is and what the event is for – in this case it was to entertain international investors – they will have an understanding and appreciation of the event. This is important because they will be front-line service staff to the client and the client's guests.

Information such as this will help with staff engagement and support. Besides, why should they *not* know all about this event and the client they will be serving?

Why the garden?

When the staff are briefed that the client has requested a private area for their guests to enjoy lunch so that they can meet up, network and socialise with each other, and that the garden has been chosen because of the splendid view, the staff will appreciate the rationale of this request and it is no longer just 'an inconvenience'.

Potential repeat business

It would raise the importance of the event if the staff were aware that this corporate client could bring more business into the zoo. It may also raise the level of service standards, too.

The client chose the zoo

It would be worthwhile to explain to staff that the client did not *have* to choose the zoo for their event. The staff will understand that other venues exist and the client could easily have had lunch elsewhere. But, the event manager successfully sold the event at the zoo and the client did choose it: they made a choice and chose to come to the zoo. This should inject a level of pride among the zoo staff.

In addition, it is important to convey to staff that are not in the business of event management, just how complex it is to satisfy a corporate client so that they can appreciate the behind-the-scenes planning that has gone into this event happening.

If the events department exists in isolation without communicating to other departments the complexity and intricacies of clients' needs and expectations, and the effort it takes to deliver those needs and expectations, there will be a failure in the understanding and co-operation of other staff.

A corporate client would have needs, expectations and required levels of standards that the daily visitors would not possess. The event booking process would be lengthy: the enquiry; the show-round; the confirmation; the lead-in... It is essential that other staff are aware of these complexities. Otherwise, they simply will not know about it and never appreciate how the events department go about securing bookings and looking after clients.

8.2.3.1 Client briefing

It can be advantageous to meet with the client for a final briefing just before the event occurs. This can be as near as a day or two before the event day. Or, it can be on the date of the event and before the time of the rehearsal is reached. Often, the client will want to watch or take part in the rehearsal, so if arrangements are made for the client to arrive earlier, the client briefing can take place pre-rehearsal.

The purpose of the client briefing is to finalise last minute arrangements, such as guest lists and VIP arrivals. Or, to ensure that any last-minute changes to the event schedule have been communicated. However, the main objective is to receive client approval at this late stage when every element is in place so as to mitigate problems or unmet expectations after the event. If the client briefing takes place, it is difficult for a client to complain about something post-event.

8.2.3.2 Sponsor briefing

Where sponsors are supporting an event, it is advisable to hold a sponsor briefing. This can be before the day of the event, if possible. However, if the sponsors

52   THE MANAGEMENT OF EVENT VENUES

are many, are not available, or distance makes it difficult to meet pre-event, it makes sense to conduct the sponsor briefing onsite on the day of the event.

If the sponsor is to make a speech or present an award, they will need to rehearse. It makes sense, therefore, to conduct sponsor briefings on the day of the event, pre-rehearsal.

The purpose of the sponsor briefing is to ensure all sponsors are aware of their responsibilities and limitations. This is important especially where product sampling is concerned, so as to prevent conflicts, territory arguments and aggressive selling techniques.

Also, sponsors may have responsibilities, such as hosting a table or a pre-event reception, so it is helpful to brief them on these responsibilities. However, the main objective is to receive sponsor approval at this late stage when every element is in place, so as to mitigate problems or unmet expectations after the event. If the sponsor briefing takes place, it is difficult for a sponsor to complain about something post-event.

8.3 The communication process for venues

In most venues there will be a member of staff delegated with the responsibility for facilitating event clients. This would be the head of events, events manager, events co-ordinator, or events planner.

Even in venues that do not have this position in place because they do not often host events and it would not be viable to employ a member staff with the sole responsibility of managing events, somebody would assume the role for the occasion. This might be the venue manager, sales manager, or marketing manager.

The difference here is that in the latter case, the venue manager, sales manager, or marketing manager may not have experience of organising events.

Whatever the case, the staff member at the venue who is responsible for the event being organised, now has the responsibility to coordinate all the resources for the event.

One of these responsibilities is communication.

8.3.1 Heads of department (HOD) meetings

Most corporations, organisations, hotels and venues will be familiar with the procedure of conducting *weekly* heads of department meetings. At this meeting, the most senior attendee (usually the general manager or deputy manager) will ask each HOD to report on their department.

For the events department, their report will include communicating imminent events happening at the venue. 'Imminent' relates to events happening between this and the next HOD meeting.

It is important to remember that events represent a standalone income stream and should be treated as a department in its own right. Even if there is not an events department, but the event is being handled by marketing or sales, an event must never be treated as merely an 'add-on'.

The HOD meeting must have time allocated for the reporting of forthcoming events because this is a vital channel of communication to all other departments. Therefore, the HOD agenda must show events as a standalone department (even where it is not).

At the weekly HOD meeting, the person responsible for events must communicate the level of event enquiries, who they are from and what is their current status.

For example:

- There were six event enquiries received last week:

  Four were from local firms

  One was from Coca-Cola, London

  One was from the record label representing Elton John

- There are 13 confirmed events in the bookings diary, three of which occur in the forthcoming week.
- The three events this week … [here there will be a run-through of the function sheet (see 8.2.2) for each event]

First, it is important to report the level of enquiries, which are of interest in the HOD meeting due to the potential financial contribution to the core business, which is a performance measurement and should be reported.

It should be that the HODs witness the growth of enquiries over time. It will not take long before the HODs begin rating the performance of the events department by the increase or decrease of event enquiries.

54 THE MANAGEMENT OF EVENT VENUES

Second, the HODs will be interested to learn that there is a possible event with an international blue-chip organisation, such as Coca-Cola, and will assume it is a healthy budget. This level of communicative interaction allows other departments to take interest and show enthusiasm in the business of the events department.

Third, if there is an exciting or high-profile event enquiry, such as the record label representing Elton John, the HODs will look forward to the possibility of this enquiry converting to a confirmation. They will show interest, ask about its progress from enquiry to confirmation, and will already be won over before the event takes place.

In the case of the 13 confirmed events in the bookings diary, the events manager should issue a weekly update – the event forecast (see 8.2.1).

With the three confirmed events happening in the forthcoming week, the events manager will provide more details and run through each function sheet (see 8.2.2).

This level of detailed information will allow the HODs to reassess the forthcoming week's staffing levels, which areas are being used (or closed) to facilitate events, and to make special preparations according to the specific needs of each event. This also becomes the forum for HODs to ask questions relating to each event.

One cannot expect distanced staff and managers to become engaged or enthusiastic about events in their venue if they do not know about them (and how difficult it is to meet the client's expectations).

Chapter 9

The Berners one-person management structure

For a venue to effectively co-ordinate (and communicate) all elements necessary for the success of an event, the events manager must be in possession of all information relating to each event.

For this reason – the vital need to collate and possess all relevant and comprehensive information – a venue which hosts events should have the structure where *one* staff member handles each event in its entirety *per event*.

This follows the same principle as organisations that structure their employees so that one person is responsible for a client account – an account manager.

So, the venue's events manager is solely responsible for each event, beginning to end.

If the venue hosts events frequently and there exists an events department with an events team, there must also exist a hierarchy, but still adopting the one person management structure (one person per event, beginning to end).

The hierarchical structure of an events department at a non-dedicated or unusual venue may be as seen in Figure 9.1.

56 THE MANAGEMENT OF EVENT VENUES

```
┌─────────────────┐
│  Head of Events │
└────────┬────────┘
         │
┌────────┴────────┐
│ Events Assistant│
└─────────────────┘
```

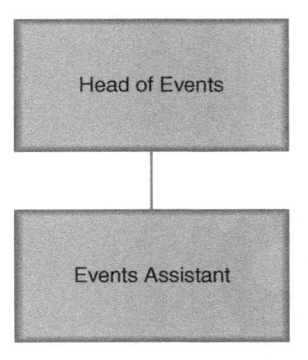

Figure 9.1 Hierarchical structure of an events department at a non-dedicated or unusual venue

In the hierarchical structure seen in Figure 9.1, the head of events may otherwise be referred to as 'event manager'.

The events assistant will perform back-up and operational duties at the event.

The hierarchical structure of an events department at a dedicated (purpose-built) venue may be as seen in Figure 9.2.

In Figure 9.2, it can be seen how the levels of business from events will impact the size of the event department at the venue. Here, the structure is less flat and more pyramidal in nature.

Where a venue hosts many events, or is a purpose-built venue for events, there will be the need for an even larger and wider team of specialists in their field, such as a technical manager.

The head of events oversees the running of the department, including sales, marketing, and staffing. They may become less operational due to these other responsibilities that go into running a department, but they will still oversee operational standards and procedures, and customer service. In this way, they adopt a holistic view, but remain directly involved with the management and running of events under their jurisdiction.

The event co-ordinators (acting as account handlers) are each allocated their events to work on from start to finish.

In a venue with fewer events, there could be just one co-ordinator. In a venue with a portfolio of events, there may be three or more co-ordinators.

What remains key with the hierarchy at all venues is to maintain the structure whereby one staff member handles each event from beginning to end.

THE BERNERS ONE-PERSON MANAGEMENT STRUCTURE 57

```
                    ┌──────────────────┐
                    │  Head of Events  │
                    └──────────────────┘
                             │
              ┌──────────────┴──────────────┐
     ┌─────────────────┐          ┌─────────────────────┐
     │     Event       │          │ Event Sales Manager │
     │ Co-ordinator(s) │          │                     │
     └─────────────────┘          └─────────────────────┘
              │
   ┌──────────┼──────────────────┬──────────────────────┐
┌──────────┐         ┌────────────────────┐    ┌───────────────────┐
│Head Chef │         │ Event Assistant(s) │    │ Technical Manager │
└──────────┘         └────────────────────┘    └───────────────────┘
```

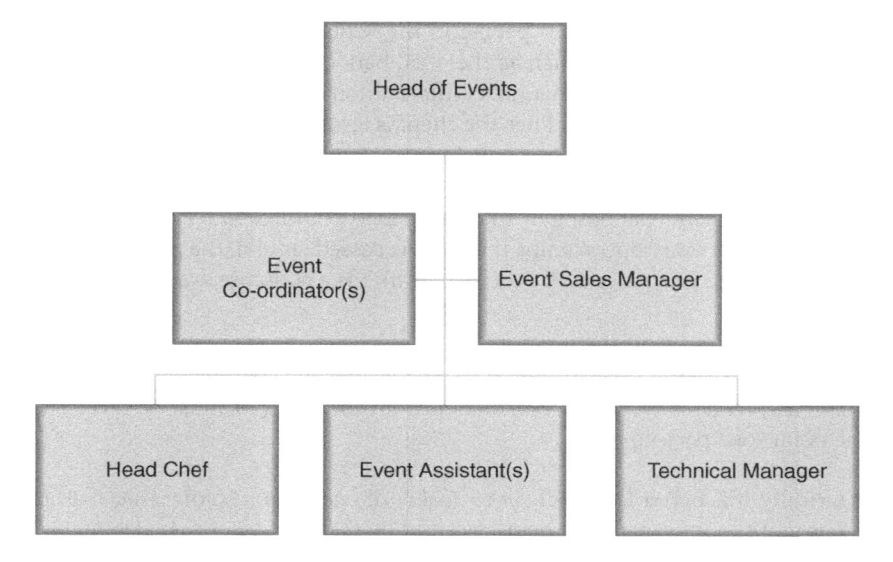

Figure 9.2 Proposed hierarchical structure of an events department at a dedicated (purpose-built) venue

This is an important criterion so that the client does not get passed from person to person. It would be inefficient for the venue – and detrimental experience for the client – for a venue to develop a structure whereby the client places their enquiry with a receptionist, gets passed to the sales manager, then has a show-round conducted by the head of events, then confirms their event to the head of events, who in turn transfers the client to an events co-ordinator. In some cases, the client might then be transferred to the chef to answer menu queries, to the bar manager for drinks queries, and to the technical manager for queries relating to sound and light.

A client does not need to know the hierarchical structure of any venue. Nor should a client receive a diminished service or experience because of it. What a client expects – and deserves – is a seamless experience from the point of enquiry to the point of exit. Everything which occurs between – the 'client experience' – should be between client and organiser only: nobody else!

One person responsible for each event is essential for the following professional and practical reasons.

9.1 Client relationship

The venue must achieve good relationships with event clients from the outset. This is valuable in converting the enquiry to a sale. This is far more effective on a one-to-one basis, where the client and the events manager develop a working relationship and an understanding of each other's needs from the very beginning.

If the client is passed to other people in the venue or is asked to work with a delegation from the venue, such as the chef, bars manager, security manager ... it can create a 'cross-contamination' of information because each department has different priorities and needs. Plus, the client is less likely to form strong relationships across a wider range of personnel.

The venue-to-client relationship is the cornerstone of a successful event and it must be built upon at every opportunity. If a client is passed around, the process of building relationships has to begin all over again, which is a nonsense way to run a venue.

9.2 Receiving information

When the venue is receiving information from the client, it must be received at one point (one person).

Practically, it is better for the client to deal with one person so that they feel confident that the information is being received by the right person. It also makes it easier for the client to have one point of contact with whomever is dealing with their event, and they will not be chasing different people at the venue.

If the events manager needs to obtain information from other departments, so be it. But, it is not for the client to chase various departments for information.

Furthermore, if a client is allowed to pass information to the venue via a range of people in various departments, it is inevitable that something will be forgotten or not passed along the chain. Invariably, this will only become apparent when it is too late to remedy.

9.3 Disseminating information

With one person responsible for each event, all information will be consistent when passed to various departments, staff and suppliers.

9.4 Onsite event management

The events manager will already be in possession of generic information from each department, such as sample menus from the chef, drinks prices from the bar manager, and the range of equipment available from the technical manager. Thereafter, it is the events manager's role to liaise with each head of department about each event's specific requirements.

When it comes to the day of the event, the *one* event manager who is responsible for the event will possess all information and knowledge, and will be onsite to ensure the right things happen at the right time and in the right place.

The flow of information back and forth must be channelled through the one event manager so that nothing gets missed and – vitally – all information on the day of the event is known by the one person in authority (the event manager).

It is also expected that the event manager possesses established relations with event providers – sound and lighting companies, event caterers, marquee hire companies, florists ... and is in possession of procurement details such as costs and delivery times. This generic information can be at hand as a guide for when a client requires, even at the enquiry stage. It would not be efficient for the event manager to spend time gathering this generic information from providers for every enquiry, especially as some enquiries may not convert to bookings.

It can be seen how valuable it is for one person to control the event from enquiry to conclusion. It limits the risk of elements being missed, forgotten, or miscommunicated. Events management is about minimising risk.

If the barrier to this one-person management structure is the belief that more people need to be involved in case that 'one' person is not available (due to sickness, perhaps), well the management procedures in place at the venue should be such that a nominated person could step in, pick up the event file and know *everything* about the event. (These procedures are discussed at length in my previous book, *The Practical Guide to Organising Events*.)

If the one-person management structure in in place, the need for liaison with various departments (or suppliers), will be conducted by the events manager. This will prevent departments liaising with each other, without inclusion of the event manager.

The same applies when liaising between the client and other departments, other departments with suppliers, and the client with suppliers. It should all be conducted via the event manager. This is to prevent the event manager being excluded from conversations relating to the event.

The point here is that the event manager will conduct liaisons and meetings with all parties, and will attend any such meetings.

It is a severe operational mistake to allow the client to liaise directly with other people who will be working the event, whether employed at the venue or otherwise, because discussions would take place outside the event manager's knowledge. If this is allowed to happen, this would be the point – right here – where the event manager lost control of the management of that event.

Even in the common situation of clients attending a menu tasting with the chef (or catering manager, or outside caterer), the event manager must still be in attendance to make notes of the comments, requirements and final agreed menu. It can be seen that if the client were to make comments and adjustments to the menu with the chef but without the event manager, the event manager would not be party to what was discussed. Apart from the event manager being excluded from the process, a menu tasting is yet another relationship-building opportunity where the event manager can build rapport with the client as well as learning more about their likes and dislikes.

A common failure with venues of all types – whether dedicated or non-dedicated, busy with events or not – is that there is not *one* person solely responsible for the management of events and event clients.

In smaller venues, a client can get passed around various managers, depending upon whomever happens to be in the office at the time. It can be pot-luck who the client speaks to, depending on who answers the phone. This not only occurs at the enquiry stage (which would be bad enough), but throughout the entire event-handling procedure. A client may have placed the enquiry, confirmed the booking, had the show-round, and *still* find themselves being passed to the chef, the bar manager, the technical manager ...

But even larger venues with a structured event team may not be fully aware how the client process is impacted by passing clients through a system and not having the one-person approach. Many venues still do not provide direct contact to the events department which means a client will first speak to a receptionist, reservationist, sales person or call handler.

AUTHOR'S VOICE BOX

I know a four-star hotel with over 100 weddings each year but still no direct line for a client to speak to the events department.

In this hotel, reception receives all calls, which is not unusual practice.

But will the events manager know how many event enquiry calls were not answered because reception was busy with check-ins, check-outs, with other calls, or was unattended at the time?

And what if the event enquiry is answered at reception, but was mishandled? Or the potential client asked a question and received an incorrect answer?

If the events team are professionals and specialists at client handling and winning events business, it is they who should receive the enquiry: this of course is the first step of the one-person management structure.

THE BERNERS ONE-PERSON MANAGEMENT STRUCTURE

Some venues evolve their events team to the extent where everybody is doing everything. This will result in overstaffing the events department because inefficiencies occur due to blurred lines of responsibility.

Clients will feel the consequence of this, and so the profitability of the venue can suffer.

It can also have the effect of distancing the head of events from the operational aspects of the department because their role becomes defined by managing a busy department. In other words, they evolve from an event manager to a department manager. This is a problem because the head of events is usually the member of the team with the most experience of events management. They need to uphold standards, devolve their experience and knowledge, and demonstrate leadership. They cannot achieve this if running the department forces them to spend all day in an office.

The one-person management structure can also fail at non-dedicated venues that host events infrequently. With such venues, the rationale may be that a full-time events manager is not required, so it does not matter who does it.

However, it is precisely this type of venue that can fail at events because of their inconsistency with the management of events, their inexperience of event organisation, and because their event procedures are not well practised. This is a mix which requires strong one-person management for efficient client management.

AUTHOR'S VOICE BOX

I visited a venue for a show-round on behalf of a client who would be holding a presentation followed by a party.

This venue was once a military building with architectural interest, so it was not built for the purpose of events (non-dedicated venue).

However, the venue was being purpose-run as an events venue and marketed itself as such, so I reasonably expected the staff to be experienced, well organised and proficient in running events.

The venue show-round was conducted by the general manager, who subsequently emailed me his proposal.

After this, a director telephoned me and asked me to attend a meeting. At this meeting, the director informed me that the general manager had overstepped his limits of authority and the proposal was invalid.

At this point, the director and I renegotiated the proposal.

After that meeting, I was introduced to the venue's 'event manager' who was to be my point of contact from then on.

So, why was the event manager not handling the enquiry and proposal procedures?

It did not take very long for me to realise this was a venue without an effective management structure, and that if the venue's structure was disjointed so would be their management of the event.

I could not recommend this venue to my client.

Chapter 10

The role of the venue

It can be helpful to recognise that there are three types of event organiser.

1   The venue's event manager employed in-house.
2   The client.
3   The events specialist – who could be a freelance event manager, an event agency, or an event company contracted by the client to run their event.

It is not unusual for all three types of event manager to be involved with organising one event. This will be where the client contracts an events specialist to run the event at a venue with an in-house event manager.

Each of these will consider themselves to be in charge of organising the event.

To compound the issue of who is in charge, there can be sponsors, a catering company, production manager, PR company, marketing company, and a security company. All of whom want to make the decisions.

To avoid confusion – and conflicts – it is necessary to identify the 'real' event organiser. This is the person whom has the most knowledge and experience of what is being organised, and it is not a static solution. So, where issues involving the venue are concerned, the other organisers must elevate the venue event manager to be the 'real' event organiser. Likewise, when technical issues are being discussed, the other organisers must deem the technical manager to be the 'real' event organiser, and so on.

This makes sense because the venue manager knows more about this venue than the other organisers, and the technical manager knows more about the technical elements. This may seem obvious, but is very often assumed, overlooked, forgotten about, or simply not understood.

But, because the event is happening at a venue, and the venue's reputation is at stake, and for the sake of the safety of everybody at that venue, it is the *venue events manager* who must ascertain who is experienced at what.

Indeed, the venue manager must get to understand the level of events experience the client has. If the client has engaged an events specialist, the venue manager must not assume, but ascertain the level of experience of the specialist. Some event 'specialists' are in the business of organising events, but may be inexperienced because they are truly a marketing company – or at least they may be inexperienced in this *type* of event. Many events specialists *do* have all-round events experience, but some hone their skills in one sector of the events industry. A freelancer who specialises in organising conferences, for example, may not possess the skills for organising a fashion show. The venue manager must understand this.

It is not always clear whether a client (or a specialist for that matter) has experience of events management. Some clients will adopt a professional stance and pretend they know the business of events. Or, they might have a level of pride where they would not admit or display their knowledge shortfalls. And, if it is an events 'specialist', they will be less likely to reveal their inadequacies or knowledge gaps.

Not all clients have limited knowledge. Some clients possess good experience of events – even if they are not the events manager, but the marketing manager, sales manager or PR manager – they might have been involved with organising many events, especially if they are employed by a large organisation which puts on a portfolio of events.

Even if a client brings in an events specialist to a project, it cannot be assumed that the client is naive when it comes to managing events. Often, clients hire specialists for their specialist knowledge, creativity or technical requirements – or they simply like to rely on someone they know, particularly if they have a loyal support or a friend. For this reason, many event clients have their preferred specialists that they work with on a regular basis.

So, it is important to untangle the knotted threads that bind these events organisers – the decision makers – who come together at one event: this would be the venue manager, the client, and the specialist. Otherwise, everybody will be pulling against each other as they seek to demonstrate their expertise over each other decision maker. When this happens, the knots tighten and conflict will happen.

Some venues only bother to understand the level of experience of their clients so as to learn the knowledge gaps and thus exploit the sales opportunities.

> **AUTHOR'S VOICE BOX**
>
> At one event, I was in the role of the events specialist and my client was an internet marketing specialist.
>
> After the event, the venue events manager expressed surprise to me that my client didn't know much about organising events.
>
> I explained that she was widely experienced in marketing internet websites, not organising events.
>
> Only then, *after* the event, did it transpire that the venue had assumed my client was an events organiser.
>
> The responsibility for this miscommunication rested with us all. I knew my client's job, so I didn't think to impart that information to the venue.
>
> Or, perhaps my client should have introduced her job title and role to the venue manager.
>
> However, the venue didn't know my client's job and had failed to ask for this information, and it is this lack of knowledge which had made it *their* responsibility to ask.

It is for the events manager employed at the venue to ascertain the experience of the client and the level of support they require.

This level of communication – the act of understanding who is the 'real' event manager – is important to overcome miscommunications. It will also reduce conflict between each decision maker. Further, it will bond the organisers and strengthen their relationship. After all, this is all about pulling together to achieve the objective of a successful event.

More than the above, it will prevent assumptions and highlight gaps in knowledge and skills.

It is important for the success of the event and its effective planning, that the event organisers assess each-other and identify where lie the strengths, weaknesses and breadth of experience – that is why they have come together for the project.

This is also an important way to identify the limits of experience of the team. If there is limited experience identified among the management team, there is an opportunity to overcome the situation by outsourcing a professional who possesses that particular expertise. If the limits have not been recognised, the success of the event may suffer.

Clearly, a bride and groom organising their wedding will likely have limited experience of organising events. They will rely on the venue to advise them on every aspect of the happy occasion. A venue manager should recognise this, easily.

It is less obvious with corporate clients and events specialists, however.

In cases where a 'private client' is organising the event, such as a wedding or birthday party, the client is vulnerable to unscrupulous behaviour from venues. They can be overcharged for the hire of the venue; pay too much for catering; be cheated at the bar; and receive little or no support and guidance.

This is not only true for naive brides and grooms, or first-time party organisers. Corporate clients with little experience of organising events are vulnerable to exploitation.

A professional venue will advise and assist the client, whereas a 'wrong' venue may exploit a client's naivety.

This is another reason why clients stick with organisers (and venues) they know and trust.

AUTHOR'S VOICE BOX

When I was the venue events manager for the London Hippodrome in Leicester Square, I often heard production companies inform their clients that they needed to bring in much more sound equipment than was already in situ.

This was ludicrous because this venue was a nightclub and had all the sound equipment it needed.

If a client was savvy enough to spot this, some production companies would tell their clients that the imposing in-house sound system was good for music and clubbing, but not for voice and speech.

THE ROLE OF THE VENUE   67

> Actually, the sound rig at the London Hippodrome was versatile enough to suit all modes of sound.
>
> Here, the sound companies were trying to sell more equipment into the event so that they could earn from equipment hire fees and commissions.
>
> It was astonishing to see sound stacks being lugged into a venue that had a vast sound system already onsite.
>
> As the venue manager, it was difficult for me to tell a client they were being fleeced by the specialist company they had engaged. Nor, could I point this out in front of the specialist company, because they would never again bring a client to my venue.
>
> All this sound … and I was mute!
>
> At the same venue, one of the largest furniture hire companies would often deliver chairs for events. After the event, the client would telephone me to say there were chairs not returned so could I please search the venue. I did this a few times, but never found any chairs.
>
> After this became a regular request, it became clear to me that the furniture company was charging clients for phantom 'unreturned' chairs.
>
> I began to worry that my venue would get the blame for not returning chairs, or losing them. So, whenever a client mentioned this company to me, I would recommend a different and trusted supplier for them to use.

Whatever the experience of the client, and whether or not they have employed a specialist events manager, it is the venue events manager who is the specialist for their venue, and so they must position themselves to provide their clients with guidance and support.

Above anything else, perhaps, a client is looking for guidance and support. Otherwise, they would do the job themselves.

Of course, clients do not have time to do the job themselves – especially if their job role is not organising events, but marketing or public relations. But, the point is that nobody can organise an event by themselves. It takes a range of people with specialisms to bring together all the elements an event requires.

Even events organisers, specialists and technicians cannot do it alone. So, a client must rely on the support and guidance of the specialists, and the specialists must rely on the support and guidance of other specialists. If this is not allowed to happen (by the principle of identifying the 'real' event manager), the system fails.

If each specialist – each person involved with the organisation of an event – places themselves in the position of using their own knowledge, experience and skills of organising events to advise others, their job is done.

This is the basis of being an event organiser – to advise others.

For the venue to perform this role of advising other people using their venue, the venue events manager must have the relevant experience and knowledge of events – including statutory and health and safety regulations. Here is another reason why all venue managers should be trained and qualified in events management.

For even if the client is very experienced at managing events, they will not know the limitations and idiosyncrasies of the venue.

And, if the client has engaged an events specialist, still the specialist will not know the limitations and idiosyncrasies of the venue (unless they have worked that venue before).

Thus, for the venue manager not to provide guidance and support to *all* clients and organisers, whether experienced or not, would be a failure to meet their responsibilities and they would be negligent in their duty.

To an events specialist or an experienced client, the limitations and idiosyncrasies of venues should appear obvious. Here are a few of the common ones.

- Pillars or columns which restrict the view of the stage and interrupt sight-lines.
- Balconies which are higher than the lowest part of the ceiling and restrict the view of the stage.
- Low ceiling height, which prevents the ability to hang projectors, lights, confetti canons, balloon nets.
- An auditorium that does not allow for raked seating (where each row is higher than the row in front, so that seated guests can see above the heads of people seated in front of them).
- Limited dressing room and backstage facilities.
- Restricted delivery access.
- Lack of onsite parking.
- No exterior lighting.
- No blackout facilities (to prevent daylight and sunlight entering the space – this is particularly important when using projection).

- Restrictions on food and drink (historic venues may not allow red wine or brown food which can stain carpets, rugs and marble floors. Some venues will not allow standing eating such as buffets and canapés, but will allow seated dining where food is less likely to get dropped on to the floor).

But, even where the limitations of a venue are obvious, each venue is unique and there may be idiosyncrasies of which a client or an events specialist would be unaware. These would include how the *flow of people* works in various rooms, corridors and toilet areas; *what works where* in terms of where the cloakroom should be located or where the bar should be positioned; *safety procedures*, such as assembly areas; and *safety risks*, such as slippery surfaces, steps, trip hazards and uneven surfaces.

> ### AUTHOR'S VOICE BOX
>
> I recently attended a presentation in an unusual venue – a historic garrison with a circular courtyard with a glass roof and a cobblestone floor.
>
> The acoustics of the venue were specific and should have been amazing.
>
> But, the hired sound system was inadequate. The sound got lost and the throng of voices from the assembled crowd was louder than the people speaking on the stage.
>
> Afterwards, the venue events manager told me that their in-house system was much better, but the client didn't ask to use it and brought in their own sound equipment.
>
> Is this the client's fault for not asking the venue, or the venue's fault for not advising the client?
>
> Knowing this particular venue, I suspect they had wanted to charge more for their in-house sound system than the client had paid for hiring in a sound system.
>
> Whichever way it was, it reflected poorly on the venue to have an event where the sound was inadequate.
>
> And, it showed poorly on the venue events manager for allowing it to happen, letting down the venue, the client, the speaker who could not be heard on the stage, and the guests who attended this event.

70 THE MANAGEMENT OF EVENT VENUES

Everything that happens at an event, reflects upon the venue.

The venue events manager has a role to protect the reputation of the venue. It cannot be allowed for any aspect of an event to have a negative impact on clients or their guests.

Guests attending events mostly have very limited knowledge and understanding of events management. What they experience is how they judge the event. So, wherever that event is taking place – the venue – is being judged also.

This means guests tend to blame the venue for anything that counts for a negative experience.

Reflecting on the preceding *Author's Voice Box* – if the sound system was not good and the guests could not hear the speeches, nobody will consider whether the client was at fault for hiring an inadequate sound system. They will simply judge the venue.

If the food at an event is cold or tasteless, the guests will afterwards talk about the poor food at that venue. They would not think to question whether the food was catered by an external caterer.

Guests will remember poor experiences and this negativity can impact the business of a venue. Reputation matters.

This is why the venue events manager must guide and support clients, regardless of their event experience: to protect anybody from doing anything that could damage the reputation of the venue. It is always the venue's reputation which is at risk.

AUTHOR'S VOICE BOX

Even the most experienced can get things wrong.

When global music stars go on tour, their production crew follows them around the globe and are in control of every aspect of the performance, including the quality of sound.

But, when a music star performs at an existing event – a festival, say – suddenly the artist's management are not in control of every aspect of the event.

This is exactly what happened with Beyoncé when she performed at the Warsaw Orange Festival in Poland. The venue was the national stadium of Poland and for reason unknown to me, the sound installation at that venue was inadequate.

Thousands of Beyoncé fans had anticipated an amazing concert experience, but left the event afterwards complaining bitterly about the poor quality of sound.

Considering that the quality of sound is a fundamental element to get right for a concert, this reflected very poorly on the reputation of the venue. The venue being the country's national stadium was of particular embarrassment to the concert-goers, who had expected more from such a prestigious national asset.

The wider consequence was the damage done to the reputation of Beyoncé as a performer.

The problem could have been with Beyoncé's management for not engaging a contractual assurance of sound quality. It could be with the technical crew for installing inferior sound. But, the venue allowed a global superstar to perform in Poland with inadequate sound.

To underline that the above situation was primarily a fault by the venue, I later met with the venue's director of MICE (Meetings, Incentives, Conferences and Events) and asked what the core business was at his venue. I expected him to say corporate events, concerts or sports events, but he answered 'sales'.

This answer told me that the focus of venue management at Poland's national stadium was misplaced because they were solely interested in selling space: it was purely commercial and success was measured entirely on the levels of business achieved – regardless of what that business was. Here was a venue being treated as a warehouse to fill with whatever could be put inside.

In commercial business terms, this may be acceptable. But, not when it comes to the other elements of venue management – quality of events; quality of guest experiences at the event; profile of events; profile of the venue; professionalism; the right events for the qualities of the venue; providing a service; client management…

Yes, a sales manager could answer that question with the word 'sales'. But, a venue manager must consider the reputation of the venue and its profile in the community – especially if that venue manager is employed at a national stadium.

It can be seen from this scenario how the wrong focus of attention had allowed substandard services to creep inside that venue.

72 THE MANAGEMENT OF EVENT VENUES

Elements for which a venue is responsible:

- cleanliness and hygiene
- service standards and the quality of service
- presentation and aesthetics
- condition of the venue
- external appearance, including gardens, grounds and exterior lighting
- maintenance
- in-house catering
- in-house sound and lighting
- safety/risk assessment
- security and crowd management
- fire prevention
- legal compliance
- capacity levels
- staffing
- providing guidance to clients.

Most of the above elements are legal requirements for the venue. Where there is no legal requirement, if something were to go wrong, it is usual for the law to be applied to whatever did go wrong: there is no escaping the seriousness of managing an event venue.

It is not fun to be a venue manager. It is a responsibility.

There are elements for which it could be thought a venue may not be responsible, such as hired-in facilities, external caterers, and hired-in staff. But even here it would be a mistake to consider that the venue is not responsible for any such elements not provided by the venue.

The venue manager must be involved with hired-in elements so as to know what is arriving to the venue, when it should be delivered, and from whom. Delivery of items must be anticipated, as must receiving goods and storing goods, foods, valuables and equipment. It may require staff to accept deliveries and move items around the venue, and storage requirements may need to be arranged.

So, it is still the venue manager's duty to get involved with hired-in elements.

The venue is responsible for the safety of staff, contractors and guests, and the venue is a key element in the success of the event. This means that whatever happens at the venue is a risk to the success of any event held there, and potentially a risk to the people within it. Thus, every element – even the hired-in elements – must first be approved by the venue events manager.

Furthermore, considering that every element of an event impacts the reputation of the venue, every element has to be considered as the responsibility of the venue.

This is why good venues, which are protective of their good reputation, will only hire services from the venue's approved list of suppliers.

A venue must know what is going on and what their client is up to. Control is essential.

Chapter 11

Procuring external services

A good venue will not allow any resources or elements in to their venue if there is a risk of compromising health and safety, hygiene or legality. This must extend to service standards, quality, and the risk of not meeting expectations.

The venue must maintain control.

As an example, to serve guests with food from an unknown or unapproved caterer is a risk to the venue because the food element of the event would now be out of the venue's control.

In such a situation, the venue must have procedures in place to regain control of the food element at the event. Such procedures could include meeting with the proposed caterer, researching the caterer's reputation, having a menu tasting, monitoring the food quality and service during the event, and obtaining post-event feedback from guests about the food at the event.

If the food provided to guests is substandard, it will reflect negatively on the venue (not the caterer and not the client). Guests rarely know who supplied the catering, so will assume it was the venue without giving it much thought.

PROCURING EXTERNAL SERVICES

For business reasons, venues prefer their clients to use in-house catering rather than clients paying an outside caterer to come in and cater the event. This is because in-house catering is an important revenue stream for a venue.

A venue makes money from hiring their space to event clients, but generates additional income from food sales, bar sales, and other sales streams such as charging for specialist staff, providing entertainment, and supplying technical equipment.

But, it would be unfair for a venue to insist that the client must use their in-house equipment and facilities, including catering. Some venues do insist upon this and will refuse the option for a client to use external caterers. There is no reason for this because there are ways around protecting the quality of catering provided, protecting the venue's reputation, *and* protecting the revenue stream.

It is wrong and unfair for a venue to refuse external services. Some corporate clients may have a contractual arrangement with a specific event caterer, or they have a preferred caterer because they have used them before and particularly enjoy their food. Often it is a matter of trust, loyalty or friendship and the client has a usual caterer upon which they feel they can rely. This is often the case with event specialists who work with caterers all over the place, all the time.

Clients (and an event specialist is a client of the venue, remember) have the right of choice, after all, and it is an obligation for the venue to allow that right of choice.

So, instead of refusal, the venue can prevaricate. It is a less negative approach and can be considered as guidance, rather than insistence. It is the 'nudge' theory, whereby the client is nudged into making the required decision.

To get around the loss of income from catering, the venue will charge the client a fee for bringing in an external caterer. This provides income from the catering element which would otherwise be lost and thus protects this particular revenue stream.

The venue should be happy with this arrangement because they have none of the costs – food, staff, etc. – but receive revenue for no outlay: pure profit.

To protect their reputation the venue can provide clients with a list of recommended (or *approved* caterers) with whom the venue has experience and trust in the service and product that will be provided. Often, these approved caterers would have worked the venue before, especially in venues where there is no in-house catering.

If the approved list of caterers is well compiled, listing reputable caterers, it is likely that the client's preferred caterer is on the list. Or perhaps there is a caterer on the list that is known to the client. This approved-list system ensures quality of catering and provides the client with choice.

If the client (or event specialist) wishes to bring in a caterer that is not on the venue's approved list, the venue can meet with the caterer to ascertain their professionalism and can ask for a menu tasting to judge the quality of food to be served in their venue at the event. If the venue is reputable, they will know very quickly whether the proposed caterer is professional and reliable. This is often the case with specialised menu requirements such as kosher or Indian wedding cuisine.

There should be no reason to refuse to explore the outside catering option, especially when using persuasion and the approved-list system. However, if a venue wishes to deter a client from bringing in an outside caterer but does not wish to flatly refuse the request, the venue may quote a substantially high outside catering fee. This would dissuade a client from bringing in an outside caterer. Do not forget that this fee for outside catering is additional to how much the client would pay the caterer, so the client might just as well pay for in-house catering and not have to pay the outside fee on top.

Furthermore, a venue should be in a strong position to persuade a client to take in-house catering. Why would a client choose *not* to use the venue's catering? Logistically, it is simpler and lessens the risks because the in-house kitchen brigade are familiar with the venue and its kitchen equipment. This makes them the best chefs to provide the food at this venue. Also, everything relating to catering would be onsite already without the risks of non-delivery, delays due to traffic, or missing items not delivered to the venue on the day of the event.

If the client remains unconvinced, the venue manager can offer a menu tasting to counter any uncertainty. In any case – in-house catering or otherwise – menu tastings should always be offered so that there is no ambiguity about menu items, flavours, appearance of dishes, or portion sizes.

It remains the interest of the venue to provide in-house catering and be in control of the food element of the event, just as with every other element. So, it should be one of the guidance roles for the venue event manager to convince the client to use in-house catering. If the client insists on outside catering, this is where the fee for bringing in an outside caterer comes into play. The amount charged for this is not about greed, but persuasion in the interests of a successful event.

Where there is a need for specialist catering, such as kosher, which is outside the capability of the in-house chefs, there is less need to either deter or convince a client to use in-house catering. Even so, the venue would still realise a loss of revenue from outsourcing catering. So, a venue in this case could either apply the outside catering fee, as outlined above, or could waive the fee in lieu of guaranteed income from other streams, such as bar or accommodation. Some venues use this method as a sales tool and would rather have a guaranteed spend (guaranteed level of income regardless of which stream) instead of offending a client by applying an additional charge for outside catering.

The point of an approved list of suppliers is threefold:

1 For the venue to maintain control of risks, legalities, hygiene, safety, quality and standards.
2 For the venue to protect its reputation.
3 For the venue to provide choice to the client while maintaining control of which supplier is used.

There are logistical issues as well. It is far less problematic – and less risky – to use suppliers who know the venue and the standards required of that venue.

Even if it is simply a delivery of items – furniture, perhaps – if the supplier does not have a relationship with the venue, the venue cannot control this element. The supplier may not deliver on time; may miscalculate the journey time or the route; may not know the traffic levels en route; or may have trouble finding the venue. These are risks that do not exist when using facilities that are already at the venue.

Another thing is that if the supplier does not know the venue, they have no loyalty established. So they don't care if they let the venue down – they have never worked there before and may never be asked to work there again. Therefore, it makes sense to use the venue's approved suppliers who care about ongoing business being referred to them by the venue. The supplier will need to protect their own reputation so as to maintain their association with the venue and continue their inclusion on the venue's approved list of suppliers.

11.1 Management of catering outlets

Contribution from Jennifer Kaye

There are numerous premises and venues which can be utilised for food and beverage services. Catering outlets are diverse and may include sports stadia, concert venues, mobile catering vans, food stands, marquees, restaurants, cafés, licensed retail outlets, conference and meetings rooms, and other hospitality and events venues.

Catering services provided may range from light refreshments, teas and coffees; to pies, burgers and hot dogs; or an à la carte menu, buffets or champagne bars.

Each catering outlet provides its own challenges for a manager such as staffing, adhering to food hygiene and legislative requirements, logistics, food storage and operational costs.

The business environment presents additional challenges in terms of rising food costs, rising labour costs aligned with the National Living Wage, security concerns given the ongoing threat of terrorism, and staffing issues further impacted by the decision for the UK to leave the European Union.

Despite these and other challenges, the hospitality and events industries continue to grow, providing numerous business opportunities and encouraging innovation, growth and job opportunities for catering outlets.

11.1.1 Contract catering

The larger contract catering companies may be contracted to provide food, drinks, hospitality, and events services to venues ranging from conference centres to schools, sports stadia and hospitals.

Contract catering may also be referred to as outside catering which can be supplied by smaller independent and local companies providing either one off or ongoing catering services to different venues, clients, private homes, events, social clubs or village halls.

Staffing is an ongoing challenge for contract caterers, especially where business demands fluctuate and regular hours cannot always be guaranteed to staff. Events is a fluctuating business and is particularly susceptible to peaks and troughs of demand.

There can also be a tendency for last-minute bookings or changes to potential numbers of attendees to events.

Because of this, contract caterers, like many hospitality businesses, may be heavily reliant on hourly paid staff employed under zero-hours contracts, and may often need to utilise more costly agency staff to make up staff shortages.

Staff employed by contract caterers can be known as 'outside', 'contracted' or 'casual' staff and may work at the same venue on a regular basis despite not being directly employed by that venue.

A contract caterer could be likened to a staffing agency, and regular staff may be interviewed and appointed to work within a venue via a catering manager who is employed by the contract caterer based at that venue.

PROCURING EXTERNAL SERVICES 79

Alternatively, where a venue does not have its own in-house team or contracted catering team, an external event organiser will directly retain a contract caterer themselves.

Contract catering staff may be required to work at different venues and for different clients in both the local area, region, UK or even Europe. This offers an exciting career for individuals – there is an opportunity to work within numerous venues and/or events and for a frequent change of environment and the challenge of working somewhere unfamiliar and not routine.

Contract caterers can provide venues and clients with flexible staffing as and when events dictate a need for staffing, even at short notice, and can utilise these staff according to business demands without having to directly recruit their own team and take on those costs.

A venue working with an external contract caterer has an opportunity to save on labour costs and logistics of recruitment.

This can present issues in terms of the consistency of staff, team-building, and quality management which can impact the level of client/customer service and satisfaction. Staff teams that are regularly changeable impede customer relationships and inevitably training and experience varies thus impacting on service times and quality standards.

It could be argued that it is the responsibility of both the contract caterer and the venue to agree set service standards and to provide guidance where necessary. Certainly, Key Performance Indicators (KPIs) such as client feedback, guest feedback and quality levels should be set into the contract or Service Level Agreement (SLA) with tools of measurement and review dates.

It is usual for concert venues, schools, hospitals and sports stadia around the UK to issue a tender to contract caterers, to invite bids for the contract within a given venue or number of venues. This enables the venue to select a catering organisation which represents value for money and quality that aligns with core corporate values.

Once a tender is won, a contract caterer will supply products and services provided by their own suppliers and their own staff to be utilised at any events within that venue. This may present challenges to the venue – a caterer may change products such as hot food, branded beverages or confectionery that may not align with customer expectations. Also, staff may need additional product training. Different equipment and displays may be needed (which may take time to install) and pricing will need to be negotiated as a proportion of the profits are allocated to both parties.

> ### JENNIFER'S VOICE BOX
>
> In response to increasing environmental pressures and in order to be more sustainable, a brewery changed their beer barrels to plastic dispensers. This not only saved space in a venue's cellar but also removed the need for gas canisters.
>
> As beer gets dispensed, the new system automatically puts gas in to the beer and the plastic self-compacts as the beer is drawn, which enables easy disposal for recycling.
>
> The new system had been installed to a venue the day before a large public event and the engineers were still onsite.
>
> However, when it came to serving the beer, the system did not work and engineers were unable to solve the problem before the end of service, leading to a number of customer complaints and revenue losses.
>
> Luckily, the venue also stocked bottled beer. But this product soon ran out.
>
> Things do not always run smoothly despite best intentions, so it is always wise to have a substitute available.

In terms of a couple organising a wedding, or a corporation organising an event, a diverse range of venues are available and each venue is likely to operate a preferred list of caterers or require the event organisers to arrange their own caterers.

In such cases, once the outside caterer has been appointed, they will prepare the majority of the food at their own premises and will likely have a workspace or production kitchen in which to store, prepare and finish food ready for service.

Depending on facilities and space at the venue, a caterer may need to supply their own ovens, hobs, cookware, refrigerated units, bars, drinks, table cloths, glasses, cutlery, crockery, centrepieces, and cooking and other appliances. This can increase costs for the caterer as equipment may need to be purchased or hired, such as a refrigerated vehicle to safely store produce, meat, food, drinks and ice. Sometimes, these costs are charged to the client or venue. Either way, this can be a costly operation and require a lot of planning, and may additionally present challenges in terms of food safety and hygiene practices. Regular food temperature and storage temperatures will need to be recorded and records kept to evidence due diligence if any concerns are raised and to comply with Food Safety and Food Hygiene Regulations.

11.1.2 Concert and sports stadia

Unlike any other industry, the hospitality sector is a service sector and an unsold ticket or empty seat is lost revenue. This makes supply and demand somewhat unpredictable and when catering for concerts or sporting events, knowing how to effectively maintain stock levels and provide adequate staffing is complicated.

The undersupply of food and drink will lead to guest complaints and damage to a venue's reputation – even if the problem is caused by the outside caterer.

Oversupply can lead to the caterer experiencing wastage, lost revenue and compromised profit margins.

To effectively plan for events a historical record of event attendance and sales should be kept recording how much food and drink was sold or wasted, the average spend per head and the staffing numbers. This will help determine future budgets, the average number of staff needed, appropriate stock levels based on previous sales, and required food preparation when planning future events of a similar nature.

Consideration should also be given to factors such as the weather and type of event as to the types of products or services that need to be offered.

On a cold day more hot food and hot drinks would be expected to be sold, and on a hot day more soft drinks and alcohol would probably be sold.

The profile of guests attracted to an event is a critical factor, also. At a football match demand will be for pies and pastries, and beer. At a pop concert it might be prosecco, beer, water, and burgers and chips.

Considering local league football and cricket stadia, these medium-sized venues may have both concourse catering and executive hospitality areas providing a range of products and services from bars and food stands, to full dinner service and mobile beer vendors.

It is common to have eight, 28 or more bars with between two and eight staff in each. This presents high staff costs and recruiting challenges to maintain the correct levels of staff, especially where events are not held very often at a venue.

Some sporting venues will hold other events such as tribute nights, concerts, meetings and conferences to optimise business levels and thus staffing issues will vary venue to venue depending on whether staff are given a reliable source of income or not.

Apart from full-time and core personnel, this type of flexible employment is normally desirable for students, those who desire a second job, those who want causal hours, or retirees wanting to work on occasion.

Concert venues may hold events more regularly and therefore may not experience staffing issues as much as sports stadia, as regular hours may be guaranteed providing staff with a regular source of employment in comparison.

Staff therefore tend to be hourly paid, contracted under zero-hour contracts and may be allocated shifts at very short notice. This presents problems if large numbers of staff are required, making staff shortages commonplace in the industry which further impacts on service standards and venue reputation. Agency staff may also need to be used to supplement gaps in the workforce.

JENNIFER'S VOICE BOX

I was once asked by a large contract caterer to work at a different football stadium to normal, which required me to travel from Essex to London.

When I arrived at the stadium, I was allocated my first Stand Manager shift responsible for three bars during match day, with one bar being the busiest in the ground.

In total, I was responsible for 18 staff members who were required to cook hot food such as pies, hot dogs and chips, and to serve drinks to customers.

Across the three bars only two of the 18 staff had ever worked at that stadium previously and the rest of the staff were supplied by an agency.

As I did not have time to train them all, I briefed one member of staff in each bar empowering them as the team leader who was then required to communicate to the rest of their team how to cook and prepare food and drinks and how to use the till system.

Service was intense, but as the bars only open pre-match and up to the end of half-time, humour helped the team members survive the shift, and customers were patient and understanding.

At times like that, I remind staff that there is no need to panic or buckle under the pressure as eventually the shift will be over and they will have survived the shift – proving that working under pressure is a valuable skill to develop during shifts such as these.

11.1.3 Restaurants and bars

Restaurants, cafes and bars provide customers with multiple options depending on the purpose of the customers' visit, their budget, the occasion, their loyalty to a brand, or even mere convenience.

Operating this type of venue requires purchasing or leasing a premises resulting in higher operating costs alongside payable rates and utilities.

As well as securing a suitable venue, competition in the local area should be analysed to identify the type of food and beverages already offered, and pricing to determine where the new business fits into the marketplace, what product to offer and at what price points.

A kitchen will be a necessity as food will need to be prepared, cooked and served onsite, appropriate licences will need to be held for alcohol service, playing music, live performances, television screens and dancing.

The venue should have enough cutlery, plates, kitchen and bar space appropriate for the number of covers the bar or restaurant is capable of holding, and capacity should be monitored for health and safety, fire legislation requirements, and public liability insurance should a claim be made against the venue.

Food Allergen Labelling legislation (the EU Food Information for Consumers Regulation) places responsibility on hospitality businesses to display and be able to advise on the 14 allergens present in food served.

It is also common practice for food businesses to provide a more expansive menu in terms of dietary requirements such as gluten-free, dairy-free and sugar-free; lower-fat options, and vegetarian and vegan options, as consumerism determines demand of a particular brand and therefore a venue should be responsive to customer needs and trends.

In a bid to gain loyalty and a higher proportion of the available market, larger branded chains tend to offer ongoing discounts and other special offers such as buy-one-get-one-free, early-bird offers for those dining or drinking outside peak times, and special fixed-price menus. While these tactics may entice customers to a restaurant or bar, long-term discounting can damage both profitability and customer perception, and it can be difficult to revert back to original pricing.

The menu may change daily, weekly or seasonally, and menu design should take this into consideration.

If a menu is to change frequently, then it is advised to write the food and drink on chalk boards, or to print it on card; a menu that will be used for a number of weeks or months will most likely be professionally printed, laminated or presented in a display book for durability.

The menu and drink items should be reviewed regularly for profitability, availability and popularity, and any items not producing the desired profit or not selling well should be removed from the menu or adapted to increase popularity and profitability.

Promotions, specials, and the use of staff up-selling can increase the popularity of a menu item, and reducing the portion size, the number of ingredients, or sourcing a cheaper supplier can improve the profitability margins of a menu item.

A range of beverages should be offered to meet various customer demands and the type of venue will determine how expansive this is.

A café may serve multiple hot drinks and soft drinks, but may decide not to serve alcohol. A branded restaurant chain may offer numerous soft drinks, a basic range of wines and other alcoholic beverages, while a fine dining restaurant may have an extensive wine list and offer a variety of spirits, aperitifs and liqueurs, ranging from recognised affordable brands to luxury brands.

When considering what range to stock, thought should be given to the value and affordability of stock which may not necessarily be regularly consumed; for instance, stocking dozens of bottles of wine and expensive champagne may offer customers good choice, but may remain in stock for lengthy periods. It is harmful to the cash flow of a business to outlay for stock and hold it for long periods before it is sold and achieves a return into the business.

11.1.4 Conferences, meetings and small events

There are a range of venues available for private hire and/or which offer events for the general public to attend.

These vary from conference centres to hotels, castles and village halls; all of which provide different facilities and services.

Not all venues provide in-house catering and may require a caterer to be appointed, whether this is from a list of preferred caterers or one of the customers' choosing.

It is typical for such venues to cater for breakfast meetings or conferences offering either a breakfast buffet or pastries, teas and coffees, and buffet or plated lunches and dinners.

In the case of a buffet, all food items must be labelled to help customers make informed choices and for allergen advice. Staff should monitor the buffet and advise kitchen staff long before the item runs out if more is needed.

A client will normally provide their own seating plan which the venue staff will use to set up tables and/or seating. A number of seating styles may be required such as theatre-style, whereby all seats face a stage or lectern with no tables; cabaret-style, with seats placed around one side of a table facing the front which is used for a conference with activities or a performance; or banqueting-style, with 8–12 chairs around a round table, normally used for formal dinners and celebrations.

As these types of venues may hold events for large numbers of people, mass catering is necessary and meals will either be placed on a buffet for attendees to help themselves or plated service whereby the kitchen team will plate meals for one table at a time.

This requires event timings to be communicated to both the service staff and kitchen brigade as service needs to be adapted to these timings to ensure that the meeting, conference or event runs to time.

This can put pressure on the kitchen and thus food may be prepared in advance and reheated for service with hot food often being held in a hot-hold unit, hot cupboard, or bain-marie. Cold items such as salads and desserts may be pre-plated and kept on a trolley in the fridges until service, when waiting staff will take plates directly from the trolley from the kitchen (or another service area where the kitchen is not nearby, such as a side room or corridor) to a table as directed by the Conference and Banqueting/Events Manager or Supervisor.

For food service, the commodity most required by chefs is the availability of space for the preparation of food.

Food is normally served one table at a time to ensure that all tables are served quickly, efficiently and correctly according to the table plan.

Hot food will be plated by chefs one table at a time and service is more efficient and professional if one table can be served all at once; for example, five waiting staff carrying two plates each for a table of ten, with all ten plates being put down on the table simultaneously.

Clearing this type of service will require trolleys or service stations to be set up, and only when every guest on a table has finished their meal should the team clear that table.

Empty plates should never be stacked on the table, as this looks unprofessional. Instead, one plate should be balanced on the wrist and food scraps scraped from this plate onto another plate held flat on top of the fingers. Cutlery should also be stacked on this latter plate.

All remaining plates should be balanced on top of the plate on the palm and then taken to the service station, trolley or kitchen.

Once the main course has been cleared, the condiments and any unused cutlery should be removed from the table.

Then, the dessert cutlery is put in place for the sweet course.

The same applies to buffet service, but depending on client requirements plates may be cleared from individuals if on different courses from one another.

For plated service, food choices from a set menu are normally given in advance to simplify service and a list of dietary requirements recorded so the service team and kitchen brigade are aware of which table or customer has ordered a special dish to avoid any confusion. It is vital to get this correct because of food allergies and dietary preferences.

Depending on formalities, the client, venue or caterer may have a list with guest names and what dish each has ordered, or a table plan identifying how many meals of each type are required at which tables. Otherwise, orders can be recorded on a place card with the guest's name. Some guests may forget what they have ordered, so this may overcome any issues and spare meals should be prepared in case of any spillages or if a customer requests a different meal or an allergy becomes known.

A separate bar team will normally be responsible for drinks orders to avoid disruption to food service and this team may also operate a table service for drinks and wines.

11.1.5 Security

Venue security has always been a necessary management responsibility, especially with large volumes of people gathering and the risk potential of incidents occurring from mob behaviour, violence, drug and alcohol consumption, or public disturbances.

Due to terror attacks across the UK and Europe, further security measures have been put in place such as bag searches, preventing entry of liquids and chemicals, body scanning and drug checks.

While inconvenient to guests, such measures cannot be ignored by managers and a security team should be appointed at venues where there are large crowds and also where late-night drinking takes place. Security checks can reassure venue guests and visitors.

Police and councils require to be informed about events that require road closures or crowd management.

Each venue should have its own risk assessment, accident reporting, and evacuation procedures in place and all staff must be informed and trained in these.

Car parks should ideally be located away from the main building to minimise risk of car bomb attacks, and bollards, statues or planters should be located around the building to block any vehicle that may drive into the premises to cause structural damage.

The 'Run and Hide' principles should also be considered when under threat from a terrorist attack and no attempt should be made to tackle perpetrators.

> **JENNIFER'S VOICE BOX**
>
> Following the terrorist attack on the Ariana Grande concert at the Manchester Arena in 2017, a security team and sniffer dogs were brought in to assess security procedures and to train the events stewards in bomb prevention.
>
> This was reassuring for all venue staff.
>
> Unfortunately a fake bomb from one of the training exercises was left in the public toilets. This was discovered by one of the bar supervisors doing a venue check five minutes before the doors were due to be opened for an event.
>
> If a visitor had found the fake bomb it could have led to widespread panic and event cancellation, which would have been damaging to the venue's reputation for its approach to security measures.

11.2 Guiding the client

It is always less risky for all parties to use in-house services, and it is up to the venue to guide their clients to understand this – or at least deter their clients from using external service providers where it is not necessary.

Weddings in particular tend to use external service providers: the bride's mother normally chooses the florist; there is often a relative or friend who makes the cake; and the DJ may be a friend of the bride's uncle.

It may make sense to the 'client' (in the case of weddings, the client is a private individual – bride; bride and groom; bride's mother – but a client, nonetheless) to bring in these elements from people they know. From their point of view there is no problem with getting the cake from a family friend: it will probably be cheaper than ordering a cake from the venue, anyway.

But for the venue, the risks previously described – and the risk of losing out financially – still exist. In fact, for weddings, the risks could be considered greater because the 'client' is not a professional and most weddings tend to outsource from personal contacts to save money. It must be remembered that wedding 'clients' are paying the bill from their pocket, not a corporate account, so the drive to save expenditure is personal.

If the venue has control procedures in place, it must treat weddings in the same way as all clients.

Therefore, the wedding client must be guided, persuaded, deterred.

It cannot be emphasised enough that wedding clients are emotionally involved with the event. In addition, in most cases they will not have experience in events management, booking venues, nor procurement and outsourcing.

It should be clear then, for a venue not to allow a wedding client to take control over some of the elements that go into the success of a wedding event.

But because emotion is a wedding client's prerogative, sensitivity must be deployed by the venue manager. In many cases it is as easy as explaining the risks and assuring the client that it is the venue's job to take care of all the details. After all, the venue's priority is to ensure that the clients have an enjoyable day: why should they be stressing about deliveries and such things?

The approved suppliers list is the leverage mechanism here. Wedding clients with little or no event-organising experience are susceptible to the venue's knowledge, experience and advice. Really, the client is looking for flexibility and that right of choice.

The approved suppliers list will provide them with a say in how their wedding runs.

It should be emphasised that all the suppliers on the list are tested, trustworthy and have experience at the venue. There is no risk. And, in the case of disc jockeys, the approved list ensures that they are licensed.

PROCURING EXTERNAL SERVICES

Okay, the venue will take control and responsibility for all aspects of the wedding. Where the client cannot be persuaded and is bringing in elements for themselves, such as the cake or the DJ, control procedures must be introduced.

These procedures are the same as with other events. The venue manager must meet with the suppliers, establish a relationship with them, and let them know the venue's expectations of them. Emails should be exchanged so that there is no ambiguity and the agreements are more than verbal. Research can be done as to the professionalism of these suppliers.

So, the venue needs control of all suppliers to the wedding. However, there is a financial aspect to consider as well.

Financially, the approved list of suppliers for weddings – cake makers; florists; sweet carts; gifts; carriages; disc jockeys; photographers – are those who have a financial agreement with the venue, as well as the fact that they are trustworthy suppliers. Typically, the agreement will be commission-based, where the supplier provides a percentage of their charge to the venue for referring business to them.

If the venue allows a wedding client to bring in their own elements, there is not only a risk of things going wrong, but a financial loss, too.

Where a financial aspect has been negotiated with suppliers, it encourages the venue to find solutions to the problem of wedding clients sourcing their own elements for the event and losing control.

There is a note of caution to add here for clients (especially wedding clients who may be naive in organising events). Some venues could recommend one supplier over another because of the financial gain through commission, rather than recommending a supplier because of their reliability, or their service, or their cost, or their suitability to the event.

AUTHOR'S VOICE BOX

I know of a country house hotel that does allow wedding guests to bring in their own elements.

On one occasion the client brought in their own DJ. At midnight, a member of staff asked the DJ to stop playing as this was the cut-off time in the event contract.

But, the DJ had a full dancefloor and refused to stop playing. The staff member insisted, but the DJ stood his ground. Eventually, the member

> of staff pulled out the plug and then a fight ensued between this member of staff and the DJ.
>
> The problem here is that even with a client/venue contract in place, the DJ had not been engaged by the hotel, and so the DJ did not feel obliged to do as the hotel said. The hotel had no control over the DJ's behaviour.
>
> Control had been handed to the client.
>
> In this case it was the finish time which caused the problem, but in these situations it could be the playlist, the volume or the DJ consuming alcohol and becoming drunk – each of these are issues that need to be within the control of the venue.
>
> So, the DJ needs to be engaged by the venue, and must be an approved supplier who has a trusted working relationship with the venue. And, there needs to be loyalty built in: if the DJ feels there is a risk of not getting another gig at this venue because of misbehaviour, they will behave.

A venue should have a list of known or approved suppliers for everything an event may require: flowers, decoration, furniture hire, sound equipment, lighting…

It is in the interests of the venue to steer clients towards suppliers who know the venue and are reputable in their services. There are, after all, safety issues to consider, such as flame-retardant decorations. The venue must control such aspects.

It is also in the interests of the client for the venue to recommend suppliers who know the venue or have a good reputation in the events industry. It is not for clients to spend time researching suppliers in an industry with which they may be unfamiliar. Clients should be able to rely on their choice of venue to guide them and make recommendations.

Guests will reflect positively on a venue where the event was good and successful. If things ran smoothly or were particularly impressive it becomes valuable promotion for the venue – the venue is on display at an event, after all.

But, if things go wrong – if the sound system is inadequate, the staff are surly, or the food is not good – the guests will think poorly of the venue. This will result in poor perception, bad reviews, ill word-of-mouth, less repeat business and harm to winning new business.

This is why the venue event manager cannot allow any element to be wrong. They must know what is going to happen. They must know who is supplying what. And, they must provide guidance and support to their clients.

Chapter 12

Winning business and retaining clients

A venue is in the business of attracting clients.

So, it must approach marketing from the client's point of view.

There are two ways of looking at this:

1. How will a *client* find the venue – reactive marketing.
2. How will the *venue* find a client – proactive marketing.

12.1 Reactive marketing

The traditional methods of reaching prospect clients – methods such as the venue website and venue brochure, and appearing in venue directories – are *reactive* marketing tools, whereby the venue has already produced a website, a brochure or a directory listing and is going to no more effort to attract a client. The client, therefore, is doing the work and is active in looking at the website, obtaining the brochure or searching through venue directories.

With reactive marketing methods there is no personal contact between the venue and the potential client. This means that the venue must take care to provide clear, concise and comprehensive information for potential clients.

The client in this situation is not asking questions but searching for answers, such as the venue's location, its style, its suitability for their event, the capacity of its spaces and what technical equipment is in situ.

With reactive marketing, a venue must anticipate answers to unasked questions.

If the information provided by the venue is not clear, concise and comprehensive, or is misleading, then the client will proceed to the next website, venue brochure or directory listing. This is their choice and there is nothing a venue can do about it. They will not even know about it.

So, a venue can lose potential clients quicker and easier than gaining them.

Choice is abundant – as previously discussed, events are happening in all manner of venues so a client has a wide range from which to choose. This is especially true where the event brief is flexible with location.

Clients – particularly event organisers and venue finders – are looking for reasons to eliminate venues from their wide search. This is the most effective way of narrowing a mass of choice. But, the elimination must be quick. A venue searcher will not stop to decipher information; they will not take time to search for what they need; they will not take time to wade through text ... They want a quick 'yes' or 'no' as to the venue's suitability for their event.

The easiest and most efficient information to understand a venue's suitability is its capacity. This needs to be the upfront tell-tale statistic for every venue to reveal. If it is too small to host the anticipated number of guests, it can be eliminated from the search.

Some venues may hide their capacity and bury it somewhere in the brochure or website. Some do not reveal their capacity at all. They believe that all enquiries are welcome. However, it is a clear signal of unprofessionalism if that most vital statistic is missing or not obvious. A professional and experienced venue will understand the need for a searcher to see this information immediately. If the venue is not big enough, it is not big enough! What is the secret?

For this reason, many event organisers will move on to the next venue in their search if the capacity is not immediately visible.

It can be seen, therefore, that it is a mistaken belief to think all enquiries are welcome because a proportion of enquiries will not bother to bring their enquiry to the venue if the information is not clear and evident. How is a venue going to measure how many enquiries they did *not* get because of this?

Ironically, it is exactly the type of enquiries a venue wants that they will not get – the professional event organisers and venue searchers.

Note: Venues must show the capacity for each space or room in the venue, and in different formats such as how many can be accommodated for a standing reception; a sit-down banquet; with theatre-style rows of seats; a buffet; dancing; overnight accommodation.

This capacity information is what a venue searcher needs to land on. They would prefer to reject a venue because it is too small, rather than having to waste effort and time to find out it is too small.

> **AUTHOR'S VOICE BOX**
>
> I was looking at the website of a venue where I had previously held an event. I noticed their capacity was 500 guests. But the event I had held there was for 800 guests.
>
> This confused me, so I retrieved the venue's brochure from my archives to cross-reference it with the venue website and see what had changed.
>
> The venue brochure only made matters worse: there were no capacity details printed within the brochure.
>
> After a while, I worked out that the website had listed the *seated* capacity for a presentation as 500, whereas my event had been a *standing* event for 800.
>
> The problem is that a potential client looking at that venue's website would quickly dismiss the venue for being too small if its total capacity was 500. This means that the venue could lose a decent-sized event and a valuable client – and how would they know how many clients had made the same judgement?

Some venues deliberately hide pertinent information, such as charges and capacities. With charges, it may be understood that sales packages vary, and venues like to discuss the details of each enquiry before presenting a quote. Still, there should be a price guide so that the venue searcher can rule the venue in or out.

It is better for a venue not to hide facts from searchers: they'll be discovered sooner or later.

94 THE MANAGEMENT OF EVENT VENUES

The capacity of a venue should never be hidden. A venue may believe they are generating inbound business by 'forcing' the client to make an enquiry about how many people the venue can accommodate. But, venue searchers and clients do not work that way. If they cannot find the information they need, they will proceed to the next venue in the listing. This is understanding how clients find venues.

Searching for a venue is a time-consuming (and often boring) activity. A client will be looking for ease and speed while they carry out this task. It is far easier and quicker to move on to the next venue than to spend time making individual enquiries about basic information.

If a venue does not impart basic information, an experienced searcher will find it frustrating, unprofessional and even suspicious. They will move on to the next venue.

So, if a venue is hoping to attract good-quality clients, high budgets, high-profile events and the like, it will dissuade those professionals who handle such top events, because the basic information for the venue was not readily available.

In many cases, event organisers delegate the arduous job of venue searching to junior staff. A venue should not expect a junior to bother with venues that make their task more challenging or time-consuming.

With reactive marketing, where the client is doing the research and the venue has no contact with the client, it is important to convey the following necessary information.

- Lowest and highest capacity

    'We can accommodate events for between 40 and 800 guests' is the way to show that there are small rooms (40 guests) as well as the overall total venue capacity (800 guests). It demonstrates a versatility and range of possibilities at this venue. It also allows flexibility for a client should the attendance numbers increase or decrease.

    If there is only one room; a ballroom, say, then the minimum comfortable number should be shown, i.e. 500–800 guests. It would be misleading to show the minimum comfortable number as 200 if the venue would look half-empty with this number.

    Often, a venue will list individual rooms with their maximum capacity.

Garden Suite	220 guests
Velvet Suite	80 guests
Red Room	50 guests

Or, a venue may list the layout options of each space, such as:

Grand Ballroom	
Reception	500
Presentation without stage	400
Presentation with stage	300
Dinner	200
Dinner and dance	150

- Good-quality images of the décor, ambience and style of venue

    A professional venue searcher will be making decisions on suitable venues to propose for their client's event. It will help if they can make judgements according to style, décor and architecture and whether these fit the brief.

    Where a client is selecting a venue they are making professional, practical and personal decisions.

- Professional: the venue must suit the type of event and the company's profile. A murder-mystery event would suit a country house, for example.

- Practical: the client needs to ensure that the venue is the right size, is in the right location, has the right facilities, and has good service and quality staff.

- Personal: the client will judge the look of the venue and its likeability. They will be looking at the quality of pictures, and the ambience, style and atmosphere of the venue. They will see the cleanliness. And, they will be influenced by their interactions with the management and staff.

- Clearly, if the client does not like the look or feel of a venue, they will not choose to book it.

- Good-quality images of a range of types of events previously held at the venue

    If there are pictures of other events at the venue, such as a presentation; fashion show; party; or product launch, it will convey to potential clients that the venue is experienced in hosting a range of events and that it is versatile. This will also demonstrate that this venue is suitable for their type of event and how it might look at that venue.

- Technical specification

    A 'tech-spec' should be listed for items that are available in situ.

    It does not matter whether these carry additional charges. The purpose is to indicate to potential clients the facilities and services that are available. If there are good technical facilities, such as sound, lighting and projection, it suggests the venue is an experienced and well-equipped professional events venue.

96 THE MANAGEMENT OF EVENT VENUES

Sometimes, the technical requirements form the brief and a venue searcher will be looking for technical abilities as much as capacity, price or style of venue.

- Directions and/or map
- Direct contact details to the venue events manager (not reception; not the sales manager)

12.2 Proactive marketing

Proactive marketing methods are ones where the venue is actively seeking clients and is reaching out to make contact with them. Such activities could include attending venue exhibitions and trade fairs.

> **AUTHOR'S VOICE BOX**
>
> When I joined the London Hippodrome as their events manager, I knew that I needed to get the venue known in the corporate events marketplace.
>
> The problem was that the venue had only been promoting what everybody already knew: that it was a West End nightclub.
>
> I needed to show what *wasn't* known about the Hippodrome: that it could be a fantastic venue for events.
>
> I repositioned the profile of the venue away from the obvious and shifted the emphasis of marketing to its capacity and location – it could accommodate 1,300 seated guests in a central London location on the corner of Leicester Square above the Tube station. I also promoted its amazing technical features, such as the hydraulic stage, the incredible versatile lighting rig, massive sound, and its tiered balconies.
>
> I spent some time gathering images of events at the venue to demonstrate the range and ability, and then produced a brochure in keeping with the corporate market, showing information relevant to clients and venue searchers.
>
> I presented the venue with the new brochure, exciting pictures of events, and a corporate show-reel of previous events at a venue exhibition.
>
> Visitors to the exhibition were surprised that the Hippodrome 'nightclub' was being represented as a corporate events venue and it was this surprise that drew their interest… and their business.

As well as taking a venue *out* to exhibitions, there is the opportunity to invite potential clients *in* to the venue for promotion evenings (sometimes referred to as *booker's evenings*).

Promotion evenings draw targeted potential clients into the venue to see the facilities first-hand and experience the services and facilities for themselves. It also provides excellent networking for businesspeople. And, of course, it allows the venue events manager to meet potential clients and begin all-important client relationships.

The idea of a promotion evening is to entertain clients as if they were guests at an event. That is exactly what they are, in fact. They should experience the welcome procedure, badge procedure, bars and catering – just like a 'true' guest would.

This is why the promotion evening should be treated as an event, itself. Although this event is arranged internally and the 'client' is the venue manager, a promotion evening cannot be approached as anything less than the highest standard of event. It needs to demonstrate the absolute best of the venue's capabilities to clients who have the means to book the venue for *their* event or recommend it for their client's events.

A promotion evening will not reach its objective of securing future events business if it is treated as internal, or routine, or a no-budget event.

The venue's event manager must plan every detail of a promotion evening using the same exacting procedures for any event. The difference here is that the events manager is their own client – but no less important than any client.

Crucially, nothing should go wrong in the venue on the night it is being shown to potential bookers.

The venue's sales team, venue management team and venue event manager will be on hand to meet the potential clients attending the promotion evening.

The arrival and reception procedures must be adhered to, as must the quality of service and catering. There must be a staff briefing before the doors open. There must be a rehearsal ...

Usually, clients would be shown around the venue to see the facilities, backstage areas, dressing rooms, kitchens and technical apparatus.

Because there would be a range of bookers with different needs, a 'live brochure' show can be presented to show a brief fashion show, a dinner set-up, a conference set-up with presentation, a live band for entertainment. This will demonstrate the versatility and capability of the venue, its technical crew and its management team.

> **AUTHOR'S VOICE BOX**
>
> I know of many venues which carry out daytime or weekend wedding fairs. These can be successful because they attract the interest of a direct target market.
>
> However, a venue should always aim to meet the interest of a range of potential clients.
>
> Even if it is a wedding fair as the main showcase, the venue could also promote parties, the bar, the restaurant, accommodation, conference space, and whatever else is available.
>
> My point is that a wedding fair seems a lot of trouble to go to for just one segment of the events market. Surely, the day should be open to other potential segments. Maybe one of the bride's parents will need a conference space in the future, or the bride/groom works for a company which will be looking for a Christmas party.
>
> It could even happen that the bride and groom don't choose the venue for their wedding, but would like to book it for a dinner or overnight stay.
>
> I fail to understand why a venue would wish to attract just wedding clients on any particular day when it should be an Open Day for all potential clients to view the venue.
>
> Remember also to provide examples of what the venue can offer. If it is a wedding fair, why not offer a cocktail at the bar to relax the guests and help them feel familiar with the environment; or a special reduced-price brunch menu so that they can sample the cuisine?
>
> Versatility is the name of the game here.

12.3 Winning events business

The art of winning business into a venue is not down to just one thing. It is a combination of procedures which make the whole and drive the client to reach a positive decision and book the venue for their event. Many of the procedures are outlined in this book: the enquiry-handling procedure (Chapter 15); the one-person management structure (Chapter 9); the show-round procedure (Chapter 6, section 6.2 and Chapter 16); and others, too.

Clients respond to trust. Trust is demonstrated by professionalism.

A client needs to feel that their event is placed in the safe hands of the venue of their choice. If a client does not feel this – if the professionalism is not there – they will not book the venue because they will not trust their event to be safe.

It must be remembered that the client's reputation is at stake to their boss; their colleagues; their friends ... A client will not risk their job, their standing, and their reputation.

12.4 Tendering

A venue may tender for business. This is where it competes against rival venues for a particular event, a series of events, or a corporation's events.

So, instead of a client placing an enquiry at a venue and then booking a showround to reach their decision, the process is lengthened by inviting a range of like-for-like venues to tender for the business.

12.4.1 Request for information

A corporation may issue a Request for Information (RFI) to an event management company to receive information about their capabilities as a supplier of event management expertise.

The RFI would usually be in a standard format so as to compare suppliers of the same or similar services.

Similarly, an event management company with a contract to organise a large-scale event or series of events may begin scouting for venues and issue an RFI to identify potential venues to ascertain their suitability and viability – and perhaps their financial stability, also.

Contents of an RFI are as follows:

- introduction
- abstract
- company/venue profile, structure, senior team biographies
- membership of associations, professional bodies, quality assurances
- financial status
- insurances
- client portfolio, testimonials, case histories.

12.4.2 Request for proposal

Once a corporation has received and appraised an RFI, or if it is an event management company appraising an RFI from venues, it may issue a Request for Proposal (RFP).

The difference between an RFI and an RFP is that the former is a request for information: it is generic and would look at the viability, so it is more about the company; whereas the latter is a request for a proposal to be written: it is specific and would look at the detail, so it is more about the suitability.

When a venue receives an RFP from a client or event company, it should approach it in the same manner as all enquiries, except it may have to be presented in the client's format rather than the venue's preferred format.

Contents of an RFP are as follows:

- senior team biographies
- synopsis of the brief, including event objectives
- dates and event timeline, outline of schedule, gantt chart from the lead-in to the day of the event
- requirements: technical, theme, branding, staffing
- venue rationale and supporting statements
- transportation logistics
- budget
- risk assessment plan
- post-event evaluation methods.

12.5 Pitching

A venue may be invited to pitch for an event, and this could follow an RFI or RFP. Pitching is a competitive process and would indicate that other venues are being considered to host the event.

A pitch is a sales presentation and needs to be treated as such.

It needs to be professional, rehearsed and delivered with creativity using visual aids such as PowerPoint, mood boards, video, brochures, photos, artist impressions.

As with any presentation, a pitch must be professional, time-conscious, relevant, succinct, honest, creative, engaging and memorable. The core message must be sent by the presenter and received by the audience.

Whoever is tasked with delivering the pitch to a potential client should be a confident presenter and speaker, and trained in the structure and delivery of presentations.

Any presentation must be rehearsed – and delivering a pitch presentation to a client to win their event requires and deserves rehearsing. An experienced client will immediately detect whether a pitch presentation has not been rehearsed. Even if the presentation is delivered by a sole presenter and not a team, it must be rehearsed.

Pitching for business is an event in itself. The presentation team must consider how the group dynamics will work.

- Who will open the presentation – who is the confident speaker to get the presentation flowing?
- Who will deliver which segments of the presentation – who has the specialist knowledge and expertise of each subject area or department?
- Who will close the presentation: to summarise and conclude?
- Who will ask questions to the client?
- Who will answer questions from the client?

Pitching is competitive so there will be other venues pitching for the same piece of business. The same is true when delivering a proposal to a client: other venues will be submitting proposals too.

Care must be taken not to reveal who are the suppliers and providers. Perhaps at a later stage when the booking has been confirmed it may become necessary to disclose which supplier is providing an item for the event. But, at the early stages it would be foolhardy to furnish a prospective client with a list of valued and trusted suppliers – what's to stop that client from contacting the suppliers direct? Or getting in touch with them to discuss prices? Or if the client chooses an alternative venue, what's to stop them selecting elements of your proposal and handing it to the competitor venue with the ready-made list of suppliers?

Venue managers should protect access to their suppliers and not allow clients or alternative venues access to the source.

> **AUTHOR'S VOICE BOX**
>
> In event proposals, I frequently see a list of elements to enhance the event, and alongside each element will be the name of the supplier. Why?
>
> I suppose it is information presented in openness and good faith. But it is a mistake.
>
> Clients do not need to know where elements are sourced from – especially at the early stages before confirmation when a client could choose another venue and hand them the list of suppliers.
>
> This is particularly risky with creative elements which another venue may not have thought of or know where to source them.
>
> It can also happen when the competitor venue's prices are higher and the client uses the first venue's prices as leverage – and tells them where to get it from.

12.6 Repeat business

Retaining clients and gaining loyalty to achieve repeat business is surprisingly simple to do. It simply involves two crucial factors which have already been identified and discussed in this book:

- Likeability.
- Professionalism.

Getting these two elements right ensures that the client will want to come back. For one thing, they have already enjoyed an experience at the venue, and it was successful too. What else could a client wish for?

Clients want ease and they want trust. It is easier for them to repeat an enjoyable and successful event than to have to find another place to do it. It would mean them beginning from scratch – finding a venue; negotiating with the venue; creating and building client/venue relationships; building trust ... It has to be far easier for a client to go where this has been done already. So long as it was likeable and professional.

The main influence for clients to repeat their event at a venue, or to bring a further different event to that venue, is the success of their previous event at that venue.

However, the client relationship is the secondary influence and is no less important.

Clients will repeat their business at venues where they are confident of success and where they enjoy working alongside the people there.

Aside from doing the job well, being professional, being personable, and meeting the needs and demands of clients, a venue can employ further tactics to encourage repeat business:

12.6.1 Longer-term contracts

When seeking to retain clients and secure their repeat business it is a good tactic to tie them in with two- or three-year contracts.

Longer-term contracts work especially well with annual events, where the client is confident the event will happen the following year and perhaps the year after that.

It is not usual for a client to sign a contract that is longer than three years because they will understand the risk of their event becoming stale. Also, company strategies change and the event may not occur in a few years' time, or could take a different direction which requires an alternative venue.

The exception would be where there is a lack of suitable venues in the locality and the client would need to secure the venue for five or more years. Or, where the event is synonymous with the venue, such as The Proms at the Royal Albert Hall, or the Royal Variety Performance at the London Palladium.

The benefit to the client with a two- or three-year contract is that they have secured a venue and do not need to repeat the time-consuming venue search each year. Even if they were to rebook the same venue on a yearly contract basis, they would still need to go through the booking and negotiation processes.

Also, the client would receive a favourable venue hire fee for their longer-term commitment. Typically, this might be a 10% discount in Year One; 20% discount in Year Two; and 50% discount in Year Three. Discount terms vary from venue to venue.

An additional benefit for clients with longer-term contracts is that lessons have been learned from the previous year, so the subsequent years will be easier to plan. The client, event suppliers and the venue management team develop a working relationship over time and become a team, while each will understand the idiosyncrasies of the event being held at that venue.

From the venue point of view, offering good terms for longer-term contracts is a way of optimising business. It has already been stated in this book that events are closely related to hotels. With a hotel the emphasis is on occupancy levels; that is, the percentage of bedrooms sold against the amount of rooms available to sell and the number of days in a year. This makes hotel bedrooms a perishable commodity because they expire with time.

It is the same with an events venue. The space(s) available to hire for an event are available for a known number of days per year. For every day that a space is not booked it is not generating revenue. This makes events space perishable because it cannot be sold on a date that has passed and so the revenue opportunity has expired.

Knowing the levels of event bookings well in advance allows the sales manager or venue manager to measure the level of booked business and set targets for advance bookings. These targets should become Key Performance Indicators (KPIs) in that they provide a measurement of performance of the business. In this case it would be the performance of advanced bookings.

The manager can then optimise occupancy by initiating sales drives and discounts in advance of the low-occupancy periods – before they occur, in other words.

So, in the business of limiting the risk of expired dates with no event bookings, it works for venues to commit their clients to longer-term contracts.

Chapter 13

Budgeting for events

Contribution from Adrian Martin

Creating a budget for an event is probably the most important action an event organiser or venue manager will undertake. The budget is essential to the overall success of an event and is an important part of not just controlling an event, but deciding whether to go ahead with it in the first place.

Budgets are important because they have the power to control costs, motivate staff to achieve revenue targets, and inform managers on the viability of an event prior to any work taking place.

This chapter will explain where budgets come from, how they are developed and created, as well as some simple calculus that will help determine whether they are achievable or not.

Budgeting can be a bit like looking into a crystal ball: there are no rights or wrongs at the time of creation as nobody can see the future.

Having said that, experience and practice of budget-writing will begin to identify unrealistic predictions of revenue and spend, the ability to predict and work to realistic profit margins.

13.1 Where budgets come from

The simple answer to this question is that they come from whomever is ultimately in charge of the company, normally the CEO or the owner. Their job is to look at external influences on the company as well as past performances and internal data, and set targets and objectives for the following year. At this stage the financial director or equivalent will turn the financial objectives into a company-wide budget.

For instance an event company that has an overall net profit target of £3 million would start to disseminate this throughout the organisation. If the company had three event venues the temptation would be to split the target equally: £1 million per venue. However it is highly unlikely that each venue is either the same size, has the same costs or the same local market dynamics. At this stage decisions need to be made by looking at the historical performance of each venue.

	Venue 1	Venue 2	Venue 3	Total
2015 profit	520,000	1,250,000	670,000	2,440,000
2016 profit	640,000	1,110,000	750,000	2,500,000
2017 profit	650,000	1,090,000	850,000	2,590,000

There are a number of conclusions to be drawn from the above table.

Overall profits are rising by 2.5% between 2015 and 2016 (£60,000 extra profit / £2,440,000 year prior's profit × 100) and by 3.6% between 2016 and 2017 (£90,000 extra profit / £2,500,000 year prior's profit × 100).

	Venue 1	Venue 2	Venue 3	Total	Rise in profits	% rise
2015 profit	520,000	1,250,000	670,000	2,440,000		
2016 profit	640,000	1,110,000	750,000	2,500,000	60,000	2.5%
2017 profit	650,000	1,090,000	850,000	2,590,000	90,000	3.6%

Although profits are rising, a further increase of say 5% would only give a result of (£2,590,000 × 1.05) £2,7195,000 and so the £3 million target from the owner is a real challenge for the company at 15.8% (£3,000,000 target − £2,590,000 last year's result / £2,590,000 × 100).

BUDGETING FOR EVENTS

	Venue 1	Venue 2	Venue 3	Total	Rise in profits	% rise
2015 profit	520,000	1,250,000	670,000	2,440,000		
2016 profit	640,000	1,110,000	750,000	2,500,000	60,000	2.5%
2017 profit	650,000	1,090,000	850,000	2,590,000	90,000	3.6%
2018 target				3,000,000	410,000	15.8%

Venue 1 is increasing its profits year-on-year but has slowed in 2017 (from a £120,000 rise in 2016 to a £10,000 rise in 2017).

	Venue 1	Profit rise	% rise
2015 profit	520,000		
2016 profit	640,000	120,000	23%
2017 profit	650,000	10,000	1.5%

Venue 2 profits are actually falling year-on-year (from £140,000 fall in 2016 to a £20,000 fall in 2017) but the decline is reducing.

	Venue 2	Profit rise	% rise
2015 profit	1,250,000		
2016 profit	1,110,000	120,000	-9.6%
2017 profit	1,090,000	10,000	-0.2%

Venue 3 is increasing its profits year-on-year and the rate is also increasing (from a £60,000 rise in 2016 to a £9,000 rise in 2017).

	Venue 3	Profit rise	% rise
2015 profit	670,000		
2016 profit	750,000	80,000	12%
2017 profit	850,000	100,000	13%

Overall share of the company's profits came from Venue 1 at 25%, Venue 2 at 42% and Venue 3 at 33%.

108 THE MANAGEMENT OF EVENT VENUES

	Venue 1	Venue 2	Venue 3	Total
2017 profit	650,000	1,090,000	850,000	2,590,000
	25%	42%	33%	

There is a decision to make now and it is a judgement call: should the £3m target between the three venues be carved up in the same proportion as above?

	Venue 1	Venue 2	Venue 3	Total
2017 profit	650,000	1,090,000	850,000	2,590,000
	25%	42%	33%	
2018 profit	750,000	1,260,000	990,0000	3,000,000
Increase of	100,000	170,000	140,000	

The issue with this is that each of the venues is showing different trends and it would be difficult for Venue 2 for instance, to reverse a declining profit and suddenly raise profits by £170,000. Whereas for Venue 3 it might be too easy to raise profits by a similar amount to the year before.

This is where local and internal knowledge can help create a much fairer budget.

If, for instance, Venue 2 has a new competitor in the area and is losing business through no fault of their own, this could be taken in to account. If Venue 3 had recently been refurbished and was closed for a month last year, it could expect a whole month's additional revenue this year, in addition to the return from having the attraction of a newly renovated venue.

Working with the managers of the venues and using any data available both locally and industry-wide, as well as possible economic forecasting, will allow the adjustment of these targets to make them achievable as well as motivational.

A budget which is impossible to achieve can be damaging to morale and cause stress and loss of staff. A budget which is too easy to achieve can create complacency and overspending.

What tends to happen now is a meeting with the managers of each venue to explain the overall target the company has been given and negotiate with each manager to ascertain a 'stretch' target for each venue.

	Venue 1	Venue 2	Venue 3	Total
2017 profit	650,000	1,090,000	850,000	2,590,000
% total profit	25%	42%	33%	
2018 profit equally shared	750,000	1,260,000	990,0000	3,000,000
Adjusted target	750,000	1,150,000	1,100,00	3,000,000
% increase of	15.3%	5.5%	14.1%	30.5%

Each venue may feel hard done by, and this is often the case in business. But, none would feel the budget is impossible to achieve and all will feel motivated to help the company achieve its overall target.

13.2 How to create a budget

Now that each venue has its overall profit target for the next year, an overall budget can be created for every revenue stream and cost.

Most budget planners start this process by looking at previous years' expenditure and income to get a picture of past performance.

Venue 1 profit and loss		
Profit & loss statement	**2017 result**	**2017 budget**
Revenue/sales		
Venue hire	2,960,074	3,000,000
Food	1,545,500	1,558,000
Beverage	382,221	364,000
Equipment hire	32,000	28,000
Other	48,550	50,000
Total revenue	4,968,345	5,000,000
Cost of goods sold		
Cleaning contract	455,000	450,000
Food	448,195	467,400
Beverage	114,666	109,200
Other	23,400	23,400
Total cost	1,041,261	1,050,000

Gross profit	3,927,084	3,950,000
Expenses		
Payroll	2,650,000	2,709,000
Advertising	95,000	120,000
Accounting/finance	15,000	15,000
Depreciation	100,000	100,000
Refurbishment/equipment	237,085	150,000
Utilities/telephone	18,000	20,000
Insurance	20,000	20,000
Licences	25,454	26,000
Property taxes	50,000	50,000
Interest	55,000	55,000
Bad debts	11,545	10,000
Total expenses	3,277,084	3,275,000
Net profit	650,000	675,000

The budget and the actual results from the year before helps the budget planner to paint a picture of the venue's actual versus predicted performance.

They will be able to see that on the comparison of most costs and revenue streams the performance was close to the budget. Some lines, however, highlight shortfalls and this is where the venue manager should focus their attention.

For instance, there is a shortfall in venue hire and food income in the first section and by extension an overall shortfall in total revenue of £32,000. If the venue is less busy than was predicted, then logically the costs in the second section will also be lower and in this case they are but only by £23,000. Looking at the third section it can be seen that these costs are easier to predict (property taxes, for instance, are given a year in advance sometimes). However, it can be seen that equipment costs went significantly over-budget (by £87,000) and yet payroll was under-budget, as was advertising (maybe a reason why the venue did not hit its revenue target).

The budget planner can now rewrite the budget using the new overall target of £750,000 which is a 15.3% rise on the result of last year. A simple place to start would be to add 15.3% to all of the revenues and costs from the actual result from last year. As long as the venue was profitable this will increase total revenue by 15.3% as well as costs by 15.3% meaning the difference (profit) will also rise by 15.3%.

Profit and loss

Profit & loss statement	2017 result	2018 budget with 15.3% increase
Revenue/sales		
Venue hire	2,960,074	3,415,629
Food	1,545,500	1,783,275
Beverage	382,221	441,026
Equipment hire	32,000	36,923
Other	48,550	56,019
Total revenue	4,968,345	5,732,873
Cost of goods sold		
Cleaning contract	455,000	525,002
Food	448,195	517,150
Beverage	114,666	132,308
Other	23,400	27,000
Total cost	1,041,261	1,201,459
Gross profit	3,927,084	4,531,414
Expenses		
Payroll	2,650,000	3,057,703
Advertising	95,000	109,616
Accounting/finance	15,000	17,308
Depreciation	100,000	115,385
Refurbishment/equipment	237,085	273,561
Utilities/telephone	18,000	20,769
Insurance	20,000	23,077
Licences	25,454	29,370
Property taxes	50,000	57,693
Interest	55,000	63,462
Bad debts	11,545	13,321
Total expenses	3,277,084	3,781,263
Net profit	650,000	750,150

13.3 How budgets are developed

Creating a budget by simply adding an overall percentage rise is very basic, however, and it has already been identified which areas the venue manager needs to look at (advertising, for instance).

It is also known that some of the costs are easy to predict and will not actually rise by that amount at all (property taxes and interest rates, for instance).

By using internal and local knowledge as well as national data on minimum wage rises, for instance, the budget planner can start to adjust some of the costs in line with more accurate predictions. It may be decided to increase some of the costs in places (advertising) to justify a rise in revenue elsewhere.

Profit and loss

Profit & loss statement	2017 result	2018 budget adjusted
Revenue/sales		
Venue hire	2,960,074	3,415,629
Food	1,545,500	1,783,275
Beverage	382,221	441,026
Equipment hire	32,000	36,923
Other	48,550	56,019
Total revenue	4,968,345	5,732,873
Cost of goods sold		
Cleaning contract	455,000	460,000
Food	448,195	517,150
Beverage	114,666	132,308
Other	23,400	27,000
Total cost	1,041,261	1,136,458
Gross profit	3,927,084	4,596,415
Expenses		
Payroll	2,650,000	3,057,703
Advertising	95,000	150,000
Accounting/finance	15,000	15,000
Depreciation	100,000	100,000

Refurbishment/equipment	237,085	273,561
Utilities/telephone	18,000	20,000
Insurance	20,000	21,000
Licences	25,454	26,000
Property taxes	50,000	50,000
Interest	55,000	55,000
Bad debts	11,545	12,000
Total expenses	3,277,084	3,780,263
Net profit	650,000	816,152

Reducing these inflated costs to a more reasonable level allows the budget to predict too much profit of £816,152. Effectively, it can be decided to either raise budgeted costs or reduce revenue targets by the difference, £66,152. By doing this the budget becomes more achievable, but is it really possible to raise revenue by 15.3% in one year?

Profit and loss

Profit & loss statement	2017 result	2018 budget adjusted
Revenue/sales		
Venue hire	2,960,074	3,350,000
Food	1,545,500	1,700,000
Beverage	382,221	440,000
Equipment hire	32,000	36,923
Other	48,550	56,019
Total revenue	4,968,345	5,582,943
Cost of goods sold		
Cleaning contract	455,000	460,000
Food	448,195	500,000
Beverage	114,666	120,000
Other	23,400	27,000
Total cost	1,041,261	1,107,000
Gross profit	3,927,084	4,475,943
Expenses		

114 THE MANAGEMENT OF EVENT VENUES

Payroll	2,650,000	3,000,000
Advertising	95,000	150,000
Accounting/finance	15,000	15,000
Depreciation	100,000	100,000
Refurbishment/equipment	237,085	276,943
Utilities/telephone	18,000	20,000
Insurance	20,000	21,000
Licences	25,454	26,000
Property taxes	50,000	50,000
Interest	55,000	55,000
Bad Debts	11,545	12,000
Total expenses	3,277,084	3,725,943
Net profit	650,000	750,000

13.4 Return on investment (ROI)

Now that there is an overall venue budget achieved, the budget planner can begin to narrow the budget to individual events.

Again there are a number of ways of doing this but most event venues will make a prediction of the number of events they will host over the year. They will then apportion the costs above per event.

Profit and loss		
Profit & loss statement	2017 result	Event budget
Revenue/sales		
Venue hire	1,350,000	
Food	1,700,000	
Beverage	440,000	
Equipment hire	36,923	
Other	56,019	
Total revenue	5,582,943	0
Cost of goods sold		
Cleaning contract	460,000	230
Food	500,000	
Beverage	120,000	

Other	27,000	
Total cost	1,107,000	230
Gross profit	4,475,943	-230
Expenses		
Payroll	1,000,000	
Advertising	150,000	75
Accounting/finance	15,000	8
Depreciation	100,000	50
Refurbishment/equipment	276,943	138
Utilities/telephone	20,000	10
Insurance	21,000	11
Licences	26,000	13
Property taxes	50,000	25
Interest	55,000	28
Bad debts	12,000	6
Total expenses	3,725,943	363
Net profit	750,000	-593

Assuming the venue has multiple rooms and predicts they will host 2,000 event hires per year, each cost has been divided by 2,000 so that each event contributes to the overall costs of the venue.

The sales team can then calculate the profit of any enquiry to make a judgement on whether it is on- or off-budget.

For instance, a wedding with 100 guests paying £35pp (per person) with an anticipated spend of £20pp in the bar with a room hire of £1,000 would look like this.

Profit and loss		
Profit & loss statement	**2017 result**	**Event budget**
Revenue/sales		
Venue hire	1,350,000	1,000
Food	1,700,000	3,500
Beverage	440,000	2,000
Equipment hire	36,923	0

Other	56,019	0
Total revenue	5,582,943	6,500
Cost of goods sold		
Cleaning contract	460,000	230
Food	500,000	
Beverage	120,000	
Other	27,000	
Total cost	1,107,000	230
Gross profit	4,475,943	6,270
Expenses		
Payroll	1,000,000	
Advertising	150,000	75
Accounting/finance	15,000	8
Depreciation	100,000	50
Refurbishment/equipment	276,943	138
Utilities/telephone	20,000	10
Insurance	21,000	11
Licences	26,000	13
Property taxes	50,000	25
Interest	55,000	28
Bad debts	12,000	6
Total expenses	3,725,943	363
Net profit	750,000	5,907

Management would then predict the missing costs using established cost percentage of food, alcohol and wages, for instance, to come up with an overall profit for the event.

Profit and loss		
Profit & loss statement	2017 result	Event budget
Revenue/sales		
Venue hire	1,350,000	1,000
Food	1,700,000	3,500

Beverage	440,000	2,000
Equipment hire	36,923	0
Other	56,019	0
Total revenue	5,582,943	6,500
Cost of goods sold		
Cleaning contract	460,000	230
Food	500,000	1,050
Beverage	120,000	600
Other	27,000	0
Total cost	1,107,000	1,880
Gross profit	4,475,943	4,620
Expenses		
Payroll	1,000,000	1,950
Advertising	150,000	75
Accounting/finance	15,000	8
Depreciation	100,000	50
Refurbishment/equipment	276,943	138
Utilities/telephone	20,000	10
Insurance	21,000	11
Licences	26,000	13
Property taxes	50,000	25
Interest	55,000	28
Bad debts	12,000	6
Total expenses	3,725,943	2,313
Net profit	750,000	2,307

Some venues will set a minimum profit to prevent low-margin events taking place. The event in this given example is generating over £2,000 profit and so would probably go ahead.

However a small hire with no food or drink – a day-meeting, perhaps – might only raise £100. The question needs to be asked whether accepting this booking would turn away another better booking. If this is not the case (maybe because the date is close) are there any variable costs to this booking? If not, then common sense can apply and the booking would go ahead.

There can be many flaws with a budgeting process and at times it can inhibit and exasperate venue managers. It does, however, provide senior management with a level of control and comfort that the organisation as a whole is progressing to targets. As has already been identified here, there are times when the rules of budgeting can fail and common sense needs to prevail.

13.5 Venue hire fee

The amount a venue charges for the hire of their venue is dependent upon a range of factors.

Local market forces are one of the main determinants. If venues in a locality have determined their price range, like-for-like venues will benchmark their charges against their competitors. This makes sense because a client will search for venues in the locality of their event and will arrive at a decision based on a range of factors – the main one being price (usually).

However, every venue has its unique selling points (USPs), idiosyncrasies, and other variables which set it apart from any other venue. These differences may determine the price point of the hire fee and may even provide justification for an elevated hire fee.

Thus, a venue manager should understand that price is not the only determinant in setting the hire fee, and benchmarking against competitors is not always appropriate.

Where a venue does consider price as *the* determinant of setting the hire fee to win event business, it will prioritise price over other factors. When this happens it can lead to a spiral of price undercutting which itself leads to clients choosing the venue because of its low price. Here, the venue USP is its low price, which is why clients book it.

This may attract high-volume low-spend clients in the short term, but the long-term reputation of a venue can be harmed because it becomes seen as a low-cost or 'cheap' venue. Where price is the priority, clients will focus on this aspect over service or quality, and this again taints a venue's reputation.

The danger here is that high-spend clients will avoid such a venue.

Additionally, low-spend clients with restricted budgets who are attracted to the venue because of its low prices will still negotiate the prices – remember that these are the clients who focus on how much they spend, which is why they are attracted to the venue. This becomes a target market: those clients who have restricted budgets and the cost of the event is the highest priority rather than service, quality or professionalism.

A venue with such a policy can find itself continually undercutting prices to suit the demand of its low-spend clients. This is not sustainable for a business, as eventually the profit margins become compromised due to the demands of low-spend clientele.

It is also extremely difficult for a venue to climb out of this situation, having created low cost as its USP. It takes a very long time to shed a poor reputation, but also the target market of low-spend clients are the most sensitive to price increases. Thus, a venue which is forced to increase its prices will meet resistance and loss of business from the low-spend marketplace.

The differences between one venue and another may appear tangible and easily identifiable: style; decoration; architecture; ambience; facilities; capacity; suitability for the event; name; location; and reputation.

Other differences may be less identifiable to an inexperienced client: professionalism, for example.

Venues offer both a product – the space and its facilities, and a service – client handling, service standards, professional event management.

If event business is not won solely due to price (which is not sustainable practice, as detailed above) a venue must attract clients through its product offering and service offering.

A successful event venue wins business by *first* attracting clients through the door because of its product and service, and *thereafter* negotiating the price.

Location, space, capacity, facilities, reputation, professionalism ... these are the factors which attract clients. Price should be a secondary element.

Chapter 14

Guests at venues

The priority for a guest at an event is to have a good time.

However, there is a lot more to it than that.

Events are not always organised for guests to have a fun time or an enjoyable time, but they are always about having a good time. Some events may certainly be about having a good time – Christmas parties; social days out; concerts. But, even where the objective of an event is about serious business or serious causes and is not organised for the prime objective of 'fun', guests must still have a good time; a good experience, let's say.

14.1 Personal safety of guests

Having a good time is one thing, but an event guest has an expectation to be safe. At first thought, this may appear obvious. But personal safety is not obvious because it is a 'hidden' need: most event guests either forget about their safety, they cannot be bothered to think about it at that time, or they rely on others to think about it for them and hand this responsibility to the venue, client, event organiser, crew, and performers. In short, guests are complacent when it comes to their safety at events.

In a way, this is not surprising because often the purpose of an event is to allow guests to escape from thinking about realities, such as safety.

If the guests are not thinking about their safety, the burden of this responsibility has to rest with the event organiser and the venue manager.

Everybody knows that safety is an important element to think about. Yet, event guests rarely do think about it. This is a heightened risk because events are temporary live happenings and temporary things can get done dangerously.

- Staff may be working in unfamiliar surroundings – this is especially true with agency staff or in a greenfield venue such as a marquee. The staff will not know the safety procedures or be aware of specific hazards within the venue, such as slippery floor surfaces or trip hazards.
- Even where staff are familiar with the venue in which they are working, their role may change because the event means they must work differently and may not follow their usual patterns of behaviour and routine. This causes a heightened risk of accidents.
- Guests at an event are likely to be unfamiliar with their surroundings. They will not know the safety procedures or escape routes. And, they certainly will not be aware of hazards within the venue, such as unlit steps or trailing cables.
- When an event occurs in a venue things get changed, things get moved, things get covered. It may be that the fire-fighting equipment gets moved, or the emergency lighting gets covered by decoration or branding, or an escape route gets blocked by deliveries or temporary storage of unused furniture.
- At most events, elements are installed temporarily, such as lights on tripods and projectors flown from ceilings. When fixtures are not permanently installed, they create particular hazards of which to be aware, such as cables lying across floors, toppling of structures, and tripping over tripod legs. Some fixtures may not get securely fixed because of the temporary nature of them being there – in a few hours they will be gone.
- The temporary nature of events leads to the potential of complacency. Because the event will be gone within one day in most cases, some organisers may adopt the attitude of 'it doesn't matter', or 'nobody will know'. Even where safety regulations exist, unprofessional or unqualified personnel may consider it is worth the risk to cut corners because of the very low odds of a safety inspector visiting the venue during the event.

It should be noted that venues which operate in undeveloped events industries abroad may not adhere to safety regulations. Indeed, safety regulations for events and venues may not exist.

Everybody also knows not to rely on other people for one's own safety. Yet, event guests seem content to absolve themselves of the responsibility and entrust their safety to people they have never met and do not know.

When led to thinking about it, it appears strange behaviour. After all, one would not go to a doctor if that doctor did not have medical qualifications. Yet, people attend events all the time not knowing whether the venue has qualified personnel, or whether the caterer is qualified, or whether the stage-rigging crew are qualified.

It appears even odder when considering how doctors work within a heavily regulated industry, whereas event management is a largely unregulated industry. One cannot practise medicine without certifications and qualifications, but a venue manager does not need a qualification to run a venue, and neither does a caterer need a qualification to cook.

It begs the question: who should we trust with personal safety? And why do we?

It is helpful that the evolution of the events industry in the UK is rapidly evolving into a regulated discipline where event organisers, event suppliers and venue managers can obtain qualifications in how to manage events.

Evolvement is always gradual and it is a slow process of change to fully eliminate unprofessional and inexperienced practice in the events industry.

14.2 Risk management

Students of events management typically dislike the two subject areas of finance and risk management. Accounting or insurance are not industries they would have chosen to study so perhaps they find it a surprise to have to learn these subjects on an events course.

But financial acumen and an understanding of risk are elements required of an events professional, and a student should not want to omit either from their knowledge bank.

Events require funding and budgeting, and they make money. Sometimes, it requires effort and deft expertise for an event to make money. The balancing of costs and expenditure versus income and profit is quite often an art.

Each event is in fact a small business which requires strategy, planning and financial control.

Events can also be dangerous.

A professional in events management will not view safety and risk as a laborious chore, but pride themselves with their dedication to risk identification, prevention of hazards and the elimination of risk.

The health and safety of others is a prerequisite. Risk never gets overlooked.

> **AUTHOR'S VOICE BOX**
>
> At a recent event I organised, a lighting stand was erected to a height of 15ft. Three heavy PARcan (stage) lights were at the top of the stand, which was supported by three legs – a tripod stand.
>
> When conducting my final walk-round of the venue before doors opened for guests to enter the building, I identified that the lighting stand was a safety risk because it could topple and cause injury. I was also concerned that a guest might trip over one of the extended legs and knock over the stand.
>
> I asked the lighting technician to secure the stand with wire to a fixed wall mounting, but the technician told me that the stand was stable and didn't need securing.
>
> Next, I asked a stagehand to secure the lighting stand. He was the second person to inform me these stands were stable and don't fall over so it didn't need securing.
>
> I found some wire and secured the stand myself.
>
> It is never right to say 'it has never happened before'. This does not eliminate risk.
>
> The issue here is that I had identified a risk – and it may have been a minimal risk – but all risk must be eliminated.
>
> It is never worth risking the wellbeing of anybody at an event.

The venue manager must identify the risks in all cases regardless of whether an event of a similar nature has taken place before. Something may have changed. It could be a change in theme or decoration – using naked-flame candles instead of battery tea-lights, for example. Or, the risk could be a different menu; it could be the different profile of guests; it could be the change in staff at the venue. So, risk identification is not a one-time exercise, but should form part of the procedures of each event.

14.2.1 Risk assessment

A risk assessment must be undertaken for each event. The purpose of conducting this procedure is to identify any hazards, their likelihood to occur, their potential to cause harm, what level of harm, and what measures need to be put in place to minimise or eliminate those identified risks.

In situations where the venue is a green-field space or is being attended by the public (such as a music festival) the local authority and police will require a risk assessment to be undertaken and submitted before they will consider granting permission for the event to go ahead.

In some cases an inspector will visit the site to ensure that risk assessment practices are being upheld.

Insurance underwriters will also require an event risk assessment as a condition of insuring an event.

However, even if there is no statutory requirement to conduct a risk assessment, most professional venue managers and event organisers will do so as part of their standard operating procedures.

14.3 Common mistakes of venues

Some venues are so keen to do things the 'proper' way for their guests, they actually provide the guest with a bad experience.

Otherwise, it will be poor management, or that the management simply do not care about the comfort and safety of their guests.

Here are seven common mistakes that venues make:

14.3.1 Welcome drinks

Venues mistakenly believe they need to offer welcome drinks as soon as a guest sets foot inside the premises.

On many occasions, the guest enters through the front door and is confronted with a line of waiters offering welcome drinks on a laden tray. This practice is nonsense.

The problem is twofold. First, it is physically difficult for a waiter to stand with a tray of filled glasses. Unfortunate waiters will not even realise their arms have given way until they hear the clatter of breaking glass and are engulfed with embarrassment. It is also wasteful of drinks product and glassware.

Second, the front door is always a very busy and confusing place. Guests are hurrying to enter – usually within a short time-frame, so it happens all at once. At the front door there are many activities in this confined space: queues at the cloakroom; press taking photographs of celebrity arrivals, and non-celebrity guests standing to watch; tickets being checked; wristbands and lanyards being checked; guest lists being checked; security is present… and on top of all this frenzied activity at the front door, guests are presented with a range of drinks to choose from.

Most often, guests will linger at the drinks service point and meet acquaintances who are entering the venue at the same time. Very quickly, the entrance becomes clogged.

Then, staff will be cajoling guests to move from the doors and into the venue: this is not giving guests a good experience!

It is far better venue management to position the waiters well away from the front door so as to encourage guests deeper into the venue. Then, as the venue begins to fill, the waiters can move forward towards the front door – waiters have legs; they are mobile.

It can be a good idea to have a table with poured drinks behind the waiters, so that if a queue forms, guests can take drinks from the table – it speeds the service and guests are not forced to wait in line. The waiter should have just a few glasses on the tray as a courtesy to offer guests.

Just these simple adjustments to the practice of offering welcome drinks will ensure the smooth entry of guests into a venue, increase the service speed and provide a better experience for guests.

14.3.2 Opening the doors

Another fallacy for venues is that the doors must open on time.

If the event is scheduled to begin at 18:00, say, the venue will rightly wish to open the doors on time. But, in the interests of safety, the venue manager should conduct a final walk-round prior to allowing the doors to open and guests enter the venue. If this final walk-round delays the opening of the doors, so be it.

When everything is in place and the staff briefing has already taken place, and the doors are now ready to open, this is when the final walk-round takes place. It must be at this point because it is the time when everything should be ready, the venue will be in the correct lighting mode and hazards may now present themselves in low light, and this is when to identify last-minute problems that need to be resolved before guests enter the venue.

The purpose of the final walk-round is safety.

Typical issues found during a final walk-round include the cleaner's cupboard left open or unlocked; cleaning materials and chemicals left behind; areas that need tidying or cleaning; blocked fire-escape routes; locked or chained fire exits which, by law, must be unlocked before guests enter the venue; missing fire-fighting equipment; trip hazards such as loose cables – which may not be obvious during the set-up when clearly visible in normal lighting. But at this last-minute stage when the lights are in ready-mode, the venue manager may identify cables and other trip hazards such as stage edges and treads (steps to access the stage) are now not clearly visible.

It is not a problem to open the doors a few minutes late. Better this than allowing guests to enter a venue which has not been finally checked for safety.

Besides, it is not ideal to let the first eager guests in on time and let them witness a flurry of preparation, or they enter a venue that is not fully ready, or the staff are not in place.

The venue manager should always make an announcement to the staff that the doors are about to open. It is most unprofessional (but happens often) for guests to enter a venue and the staff are unaware the doors have opened.

AUTHOR'S VOICE BOX

I find it helpful to delay the opening of the doors at an event.

I try not to allow the first prompt and eager guests to wander into an empty venue with no atmosphere.

I would rather keep guests outside the venue for a few minutes until there is a small crowd. It builds their anticipation. Then, when the doors do open, there is a surge of energy into the venue and the atmosphere is there from the outset.

Opening the doors late can work to a venue's advantage. It generates a frisson of excitement and buzz outside the closed doors. Guests will gather and it will build their curiosity. If the doors open on time and just the prompt or early guests mill around in an empty venue, there is no 'buzz'.

14.3.3 Buffet service

There seems to be little error with serving canapés, sit-down dinners or banquets. But, when it comes to buffets, many venues make the same mistakes.

A buffet should never be placed against a wall. To do so creates one dead side. It is far more efficient for guests if they can access the buffet from both sides.

Even where guests will approach the buffet from just one side, the buffet table should be away from the wall to allow access for staff. This way the buffet can be replenished without staff having to barge through guests at the buffet. Besides, a staff member should always be behind the buffet to assist with menu queries, allergen questions, maintain portion control, and to help serve so as to add speed to the flow of guests at the buffet.

There is a safety aspect here, also. A staff member should be behind the buffet to prevent children from reaching hot dishes. This is especially pertinent at weddings where there are children present. Usually at weddings the evening buffet will consist of dishes heated by naked flame burners under chafing dishes with hot water. Staff behind the buffet should be aware of this risk.

There is no reason why a buffet table should ever be placed hard against a wall.

Buffets are notorious for creating queues. Nobody likes to stand in a queue and wait for their food. If possible, there should be more than one buffet point to distribute the flow of guests. At least, the desserts should be on a separate buffet table.

Plates, cutlery, condiments and napkins should be on a separate table from the buffet.

Creating satellite stations for the desserts or the plates and cutlery will disperse guests and alleviate queuing.

Many venues prepare a buffet table and feel their responsibility ends there. But, staff should constantly replenish dishes and exchange half-empty dishes for full. Once a dish is half empty, it should be returned to the kitchen for replenishment.

Keeping room behind the buffet for staff access will encourage replenishment by making it easier for staff and less intrusive to guests.

Each guest who visits the buffet at any time of their choosing during an event should receive a first-class experience. If the buffet is looking tired it should be closed and returned to the kitchen.

14.3.4 Cloakroom

Cloakrooms are frequently a problem, which is a surprise considering that the venue manager knows when the cloakroom will be used (when it is cold or wet) and when it will be busy (at the beginning and end of every event).

Frequently, cloakrooms in venues are understaffed and in the wrong place. It seems cloakrooms are treated as a low priority, probably because they do not make money for the venue – the client is not paying for the cloakroom and neither are guests in most cases.

Yet, when it comes to guest experience, guests use the cloakroom when they enter and when they leave a venue – so it is their first and last impression of that venue.

Also, the venue's duty of caretaking for their guests' beloved possessions, such as expensive coats, cashmere scarves, briefcases, umbrellas and hats is a serious responsibility.

If the cloakroom is temporary for the event, it should be sited near to the front door but not *at* the front door. If queues form at the cloakroom, it blocks the entrance to the venue and forces guests to queue outside.

There is no rule which states a cloakroom must be at the front door. Yes, it makes sense because a guest wishes to deposit their belongings as soon as possible, and will wish to collect them again when they are leaving. But, there are many venues which have cloakrooms at the back of the premises or even in the basement. As long as the cloakroom is signposted and easy to find, it can be located anywhere.

Fixed cloakrooms cannot be moved (although a satellite cloakroom can be set up for larger attendance), but the location of temporary cloakrooms needs to be planned. Remember, the front door is a busy environment with arrivals, departures, press, security ... so it is a wise venue manager who sites the cloakroom elsewhere if possible – and serves the welcome drinks well inside the venue!

The venue manager will know how many guests to expect, and will know the peak times of arrival and departure (being the start and finish times of the event). It must only be poor management, therefore, to under-staff the cloakroom and allow queues to form.

It can be a good idea to cross-train (or cross-brief) other staff and utilise them to assist with the cloakroom at peak times. Waiters or bar staff who will not be busy at the start and finish times will be available for guest arrivals and departures.

A courtesy, but also a symbol of professionalism and care, is to provide full-length mirrors close to the cloakroom, but not *at* the cloakroom. Ladies and well-groomed gentlemen will wish to check their appearance, and a mirror will draw them from this congested area.

14.3.5 Trip hazards

Many venues do not pay attention to the hazards created by temporary events.

The nature of events means cables get temporarily laid across entrances, doorways and carpets. When it is dark or when guests are distracted they may not notice a cable lying across the floor.

All cables must be covered or highlighted to avoid even the *risk* of a guest tripping. This is not about what to do *if* a guest trips over the cable, but ensuring a guest *cannot* trip over the cable.

An uncovered cable is either poor management or a management that does not care about the wellbeing of their guests.

Other common trip hazards include edges of platforms and podiums, stair edges, and the extended legs of tripods for speakers or lights.

All steps and edges must be highlighted with white tape or hazard tape. The legs of tripods must either be highlighted in the same way, or be protected with barriers or plants.

> **AUTHOR'S VOICE BOX**
>
> I did come across one venue that had resolved the problem of unseen cables causing a trip hazard. They had so many cables laid out, the guests had to clamber over them to enter the venue!
>
> It wasn't convenient for guests, but at least the cables were obvious and visible!

14.3.6 Toilets

It is a common mistake for toilets to be unclean. In fact, it is so common that guests can become used to finding it and are not surprised.

Still, it reflects poorly on the standards of any venue.

Guests do know when something is clean and when it is dirty. Unclean toilet areas are unacceptable.

Venues should provide toilet attendants as readily as they provide bar staff. The problem is that venues make money from sales at the bar but there is no revenue from toilets. This is why a venue may consider it an unnecessary cost to provide toilet attendants. Again, it is only that they do not care about the comfort of their guests. It is still about the guest experience.

An event budget should allow for toilet attendants. If not, the venue should provide them.

> **AUTHOR'S VOICE BOX**
>
> When I visit a venue for a show-round, I always enter the ladies' toilet to judge the cleanliness of the venue.
>
> A venue might not tidy the men's toilet, but the ladies' toilet is a good measurement of cleanliness.
>
> I'm less concerned about daily uncleanliness from usage, but whether there is long-term poor housekeeping.
>
> I can cost in to the budget a cleaning team and toilet attendants, but if I discover long-term poor housekeeping, I will be concerned about attention to detail in other areas of the venue – the kitchen, for example.

The need is for guests to find toilets clean and presentable – always. If an attendant is present to assist guests with washing their hands, it promotes courtesy *and* hygiene. It will also act as security and prevent the use of drugs.

Too many times, toilets are not easy to find nor clearly signposted. Too often, toilets are hidden. A guest should never be put in the position to have to ask for the location of the toilets.

14.3.7 Greeting guests

A venue, an event organiser, and a client will remember to provide guests with a greeting as they arrive to an event. It is courtesy. Sometimes, the procedure of greeting guests is a necessity for security reasons. This is to ensure that the right people enter the venue. It is also a legal responsibility to count guests into the venue to ensure that capacity levels are not exceeded.

However, security personnel are not always the most friendly or approachable staff. Or, they may not be trained in social etiquette.

Security is a purpose and, although most security staff are polite and professional, it is not security's role to act as event hosts. It would be less likely to expect door hosts to perform the role of security because they would not be trained to deal with confrontational situations. Security is one job; hosting is another. Each require different skill sets.

Hosts or hostesses should be positioned at the front door with the sole purpose of welcoming guests to the venue. This is true whether security is required or not.

Door hosts should be familiar with the venue and its surroundings so that they can assist guests with questions, directions, taxis and other local queries.

Hosts should again be positioned at the door at the end of the event to bid goodbye to departing guests. This, too, is courtesy. This is the stage where guests may require directions or taxis.

It should be remembered to have door security present at the end of an event as well, because this can be the stage where guests have consumed alcohol. As mentioned above, it is wrong to expect hosts to deal with confrontational situations.

PART II

Event procedures for venues

Chapter 15

Enquiry handling

The venue manager's relationship with a client begins before the client becomes a client.

It begins at the enquiry.

This is why, even at this earliest stage it is important to get the enquiry procedure right.

The first point of contact is the beginning of the client relationship and if the experience is not good, the client may not book the venue.

The one-person management structure is important to observe (see Chapter 9).

First, the venue's enquiry handler must be personable. Not only is this polite, courteous and professional, but this person needs to quickly grasp the needs of a potential event client. Event clients will expect the enquiry handler to answer event-related questions, provide accurate information about the venue, its facilities, capabilities, capacities and provisions such as staffing, technical crew, costs and menus. There is an abundance of information to provide for an event enquiry – information which a staff member outside the events department may not possess.

The enquiry handler must also possess the knowledge and skills to retain the interest of the enquiry for it to progress to the next stage.

Note: The next stage of an enquiry is not necessarily a sale or confirmed booking. It could be to forward further information or schedule a venue show-round.

In addition to all this, the enquiry handler must be adept at recording information on to the venue enquiry form (see Figure 15.1) in the manner it is provided by a client on the telephone. This involves an understanding of which information is necessary to obtain for every enquiry including those events that will not happen.

VENUE ENQUIRY FORM

Date of Enquiry: **Time received:**

File Code.................   **Enquiry taken by:** ....

Client Details

Name: Company Name: Job Title:

Email: Telephone:

Details of Event

Date of Event: Mon / Tue / Wed / Thu / Fri / Sat / Sun ....

Type: (Fashion show / Dinner / Party / Conference / Concert / Launch / Show)

Number of Guests: ....   Timings: Start .... Finish ....

Catering: Canapé / Buffet / Banquet   Bars: ....

Budget:

Quotes or Discounts:

Other Requirements:

Action Taken/Action to Take

                                                    Source: ....

Figure 15.1 Venue enquiry form

The purpose of the venue enquiry form is to record the basic details of an enquiry to the venue – enough to generate a response to a potential client.

The document does not go into more depth of information because details can be discussed at length during the venue show-round where the client views the venue, or at a client briefing meeting.

At this stage the venue does not have a booking, merely an enquiry. So, it requires a professional and competent response, but without asserting time and much effort for a booking which may never happen.

Note the following from the venue enquiry form.

- Each enquiry should be given a **File Code** which will remain the same should the enquiry become a confirmed booking. Thus, each event is individually coded and identifiable. This is important where there are many events of the same type such as at a wedding venue or conference centre, and where there is risk of clients with the same name (which is a common occurrence with a corporate client using a venue for a range of events – monthly committee meetings, for example. Each monthly event should be attributed an individual file code).
- **Enquiry Taken By** is helpful to record at venues where there is no one-person management structure and anybody could take an event enquiry, where the venue does not have direct telephone or email access to the events department, or where there is an events team and anybody in the department might take an enquiry.
- The **Client Details** section is presented early on the form and records the client's contact information. This information is important for chasing the enquiry, for future marketing activities and adding the enquiry to the venue's database.
- The **Details of the Event** is designed for minimal pertinent information and is laid out for speed in completion during an enquiry if it is being received by telephone.
- The **Action Taken/Action to Take** provides a reminder of what stage the enquiry has reached and what has happened since taking the enquiry. 'Action Taken' could include sending menus, or a venue brochure was sent. 'Action to Take' could include a note to follow up on a certain date, or invite the potential client to a promotion evening.
- If the enquiry does not convert to a booking, it should be noted here as to why. The amount of enquiries received and rate of conversion to bookings can be reported at the HOD meetings and is useful information.
- Recording the **Source** of the enquiry will help to measure the success or failure of campaigns or advertisements, and from where enquiries are generated. This is important when making marketing decisions, but may also show a surprising level of enquiries generated from a specific source previously not identified.

15.1 Receiving the enquiry

If an enquiry is received but the venue event manager is unavailable to receive the enquiry, the person who is answering the enquiry should *only* take the potential client's contact details. Things can go wrong even at this earliest stage, such as misinformation or mistaken rejection. So, none of the client's questions should be answered by staff other than the venue's event manager.

All that needs to happen in such cases is for the contact details to be completed on the venue enquiry form, which is why this section appears before any other information is taken.

Then, the contact details on the venue enquiry form can be passed to the venue's event manager on their return to the office and they can proceed with receiving the enquiry.

15.2 Date conflict

Before any enquiry is entertained it is good practice to research the date of the event to ascertain whether there are conflicts.

Date conflicts may be internal, such as a booking, an enquiry or a provisional booking having already been received for the venue, space or room(s).

Even if there is availability in the venue, it may not be possible to entertain conflicting events on the same date – a wedding and a wake, for example

External date conflicts can have an impact, as well. Attendances at an event can be negatively impacted should there be a competitive event on the same date – especially if it is in the same industry sector, such as two launches of car brands, say.

Also, media coverage of an event can be impacted by national or international events, such as a royal wedding, or an international football tournament.

A venue must not expect clients to be aware of the need to research the date of the event for conflicts, let alone knowing to consider the impact.

Private clients, such as wedding clients would not have the professional acumen to research date conflicts. But even corporate clients may select a date because of its significance (a company anniversary, perhaps) and not consider there may be a date conflict.

The day of the event requires research as well. Private clients may select a date for a birthday and a corporate client may take the date of the company anniversary, without realising that date is a Sunday, or a Bank Holiday. These oversights do occur and it is for the venue to identify them.

Rather than a venue not bothering to research a date for conflicts, or not reporting it to a client for fear of losing the booking (especially if it is an enquiry and not a confirmed booking), the venue should remember that a client would always appreciate being informed. This is again about service to the client and demonstrates professional ethics. A client may shift the date of their event, or might even bring a future event to the venue because of the professionalism shown – clients do reward loyalty.

A date conflict needs to be identified at the enquiry stage because it would be foolhardy to do so after a show-round has been arranged or confirmation has been received and that investment in time and effort proves fruitless.

Additionally, it is better to lose an event before it gets going rather than having it cancel off the books. It is also damaging to the reputation of a venue if a cancellation happens after guests are aware, so it is wise to rule out a date conflict as the reason to have to cancel.

> **AUTHOR'S VOICE BOX**
>
> I was asked to organise an event in Milan for Shania Twain. I began by researching the date and discovered that the event was in the middle of Milan Fashion Week.
>
> As soon as I informed my client, she cancelled the event.
>
> I lost this prestigious job.
>
> But, I did not lose my client.
>
> I didn't have a choice but to inform her anyway. It would have been discovered at some point by somebody, and it would have made me look unprofessional if that somebody wasn't me.
>
> I could have done a lot of preliminary work before the date conflict was revealed. The event would get cancelled and all my work would have been wasted.
>
> Anyway, the logistics would have been problematic for me to organise a high-profile event in Milan during Fashion Week. Venues would already be booked and not available for me; I would have had trouble hiring limousines; I would have struggled to get security ... And the press would be elsewhere, snapping the supermodels on catwalks.
>
> Ethically and logistically, I did the right thing.

140 EVENT PROCEDURES FOR VENUES

15.3 Enquiry file procedure

A venue should not consider an enquiry as a 'booking' until the client confirms the event.

Until confirmation is received from the client, the Venue Enquiry Form remains in the Enquiry File.

During the period when the Venue Enquiry Form is held in the Enquiry File the venue manager will periodically follow-up the lead and record the activity in the *Action Taken/Action to Take* section of the form.

An effective means for a venue to chase clients to either confirm or release an enquiry is to agree to hold the date for a certain period – a *provisional booking*. This secures the date for the client on the understanding that the venue manager will contact the client when the hold-period expires or when another enquiry is received for that same date. The client will then need to confirm the event, release the date, or extend the provisional booking.

The Enquiry File should fill with enquiries which have not confirmed. If the date of the proposed event has expired, the Enquiry Form does not get thrown away but stays in the Enquiry File as a record of the following information.

- Where each enquiry was generated (the *source* section on the form).

- The number of enquiries received which are in the Enquiry File. Counting how many enquiries are in this file will show how many enquiries were received over any given period.

- This information also helps identify patterns of peak and off-peak demand, and when enquiries are being received during the year. It may suggest when marketing campaigns are required to generate enquiries in low-demand periods.

- Reasons for discontinuance. The forms still in the Enquiry File will provide reasons why each enquiry did not convert to a confirmation. This might highlight an issue which needs addressing. Perhaps, there is a nearby competitor reaping events business, for example.

- Conversion rate. It is helpful to understand how many enquiries do not convert to confirmations as this determines the conversion rate. If the conversion rate is low, this could suggest an issue with the enquiry procedure or the show-round procedure.

- Tracking activity. By looking at the activity records listed on each enquiry form in the Enquiry File, the venue can measure the value of chasing clients by which methods. For example, if enquiries have not been chased for two weeks because the events manager was away, this could show why there was a lower conversion rate during that period. This could be valuable to ascertain whether the recruitment of a sales person or assistant events manager is required to help convert business.

It can be seen the value of retaining enquiry forms even where the event does not happen, or where an enquiry is not going to happen. The former may be because a client booked elsewhere. The latter could be because the venue was too small to accommodate the number of guests. Whatever the reason for an enquiry not going ahead, the Venue Enquiry Form must be retained. Only when the enquiry converts to a confirmed booking will the form be removed from the Enquiry File.

The Enquiry File is also valuable in providing the venue with a database of potential clients. This is essential for future marketing campaigns and mail-outs, such as for Christmas parties or promotion evenings. Even those enquiries which did not convert still remain as potential clients for any future events they may wish to place into a venue.

Each enquiry received is a future sales lead.

Chapter 16

Show-round procedure

If the enquiry is handled efficiently by the venue event manager and the venue is available on the date of the event, a potential client will wish to view the venue for themselves, meet the venue manager and discuss the event in greater detail. This initial viewing of the venue is the *show-round* or *recce* (reconnaissance).

The show-round would likely be the first face-to-face contact between the venue manager and a client.

Personality will be a major contributory factor during this first meeting. If for whatever reason the client does not get on with the venue event manager – i.e. the person in charge of the success of the event – then the client will not book the venue.

The show-round is also the client's first impression of the venue – not only the physical appearance of its style and décor, but how well it is run, and the experience and professionalism of its events manager.

A show-round of the venue is vital for the client (the 'client' of a venue can be an event organiser, event agent, event company or direct client) so they can make an informed decision about using a venue for their event.

SHOW-ROUND PROCEDURE

> **AUTHOR'S VOICE BOX**
>
> At the show-round of a venue I was considering to use for a launch party, I noticed a smart new apartment building adjacent to the car park.
>
> When I mentioned to the venue manager my concerns of noise because my event would run into the early hours, with music inside and smokers outside, he was flippant and said, 'It doesn't matter, don't worry about that; we were here first.'
>
> I chose not to contribute any upset for the residents in that apartment block and so I did not book that venue.
>
> I also wasn't comfortable to bring the events industry into disrepute by making an event a problem for other people who live nearby the venue.
>
> Plus, I was wary of the risk if any residents were to complain about the noise at my event: I could have the police attending the event to demand the music stops or the venue closes. This would cause problems on the night, but also my client might take a negative view of me booking a venue where the police turn up to close us down! I don't welcome blame.
>
> Stacking it up, it was better to find an alternative venue for that event.

A show-round is also the first opportunity for a venue manager to show off and display the venue to secure a client. This is so important that there should be procedures in place for each show-round, just like any other live happening.

- All heads of department should be informed the day before the show-round, so as to ensure all departments are aware and prepared that a client will be in the building to make a decision about placing business there.
- On the day of the show-round, the events manager must ensure all areas are ready before the time the client is due to arrive to the venue. It is not enough to expect heads of department to ready their areas – they have other priorities and demands. It must be treated as an event, which means the events manager must *check* all areas of the venue on the day of the show-round.
- A sound and/or lighting technician should be available to demonstrate to the client the lighting, sound, projection and other technical facilities.
- The venue should be presented in the correct 'mode' for the type of event that the client is looking to place in to the venue. This mode is how the venue would be presented for a fashion show, presentation, party, stage production,

product launch, or other type of event depending on the nature of the enquiry. It is important for a client to see and feel how a venue will look during their event. Pictures help, but the show-round is not for 'showing' how a venue can look, it is about demonstrating the venue to a client while the client is onsite.

- The show-round is a real sales opportunity and should not be treated as merely a prospect chance of business.

- As with any live happening, the events manager should do a final walk-round of the venue before the client arrives to view it:

    - to check for cleanliness of all areas

    - to identify any problems (dirty areas; maintenance issues; blown light-bulbs; cleaning equipment left out)

    - to ensure that staff are not lounging in groups for breaks or lunch

    - to ensure that the technician is in place and brief him on the specific requirements of this potential client and their event.

- If the venue is dark or windowless (such as a nightclub) it can be a stark contrast for a client entering from the outside. This can be counteracted with fresh flowers in reception, which brings a little of the outside into the venue.

- Ensure that there is a quiet space or room available in which to have a discussion with the client.

- Offer tea, coffee and water – this is a personal interaction, after all. Demonstrate hospitality and courtesy because the client has taken time and effort to travel to the venue.

Venue show-rounds are essential for the client/venue relationship. Good communication is key to winning a client and making their event a success, and it begins at this first meeting.

This first meeting is also when the venue manager has the opportunity to ascertain the event experience of the client, their expectations and their needs. The venue manager has the opportunity to learn about their client and understand whether they will need to provide substantial guidance.

Essentially (but not only) the show-round is a sales tool. It is the opportunity to convert an enquiry to a sale.

If the show-round is unprepared and unprofessional the enquiry will not convert to a sale.

However, it is a poorly managed venue that considers the show-round as a sales opportunity first and foremost.

The *salesy* approach is obvious to recognise from the outset:

- the venue manager adopts a 'sales patter' to the show-round
- the venue manager will tend to disparage competitor venues
- the venue manager will promise everything to the client, merely to achieve the sale. Clients distrust this approach because it is likely the venue will not deliver, or even not remember what they had promised.

Those venues which do treat the show-round as a sales opportunity first and foremost, tend not to be honest with their clients. An experienced client or events specialist will recognise this.

Actually, the approach of the venue manager should be to impart trust. A client will never book a venue if it is not suitable, so it is foolhardy to 'sell' the venue to a client. If the venue is suitable for the event and the client trusts in the event manager, the sale will happen.

Always, the venue manager should guide a client, which is why it can be important to ascertain the client's experience in events. Some clients may hide their experience to see whether a salesman trips himself up. But, it is not helpful to the relationship to attempt to teach an experienced client.

Guiding a client also means being honest with them that some requirements may not work at the venue. The venue manager should demonstrate care for the reputation of the venue, which means not allowing anything and everything to happen, just to achieve the sale.

If an event is not going to suit the venue it will result in a wrong event. It is better not to have the event, than to have a wrong event.

If the venue is not right for the event, due to its style, size or other logistical factors, then it would be impossible to make right.

No venue manager should ever allow a wrong event to happen in their venue. It will let down the client, reflect poorly on the venue, result in conflict and bill-wrangling, and harm the reputation of the venue for achieving future business and repeat business.

The point of the show-round is to present a quality venue to a client. The client should feel informed, not sold-to.

Chapter 17

Confirmation and contract procedure

If the venue show-round was successful, the venue will receive notification from the client that the event is going ahead – confirmation will be received.

At this point, the date of the confirmed event should be marked in the venue calendar or the provisional hold should be converted to a confirmed booking. Updating the venue calendar is important so as to prevent double bookings and overbookings. Similarly, if an event cancels, the venue calendar must be updated to show the space is now available to sell.

Some venues use colours or symbols in their venue calendar to denote **enquiries**, **provisional** bookings, **confirmed** bookings and **cancelled** bookings.

When an enquiry gets converted to a confirmation, the Enquiry Form gets transferred to the Client File (see Chapter 19).

17.1 Venue contract (Appendix II)

At the point of receiving confirmation the venue will raise a venue hire contract.

It should be remembered that a contract protects both parties and should be both balanced and equal towards both parties. It would be unethical practice for a venue to stipulate unreasonable and unfair clauses.

Appendix II provides an example of a venue hire contract. However, the main points to include are as follows.

- Date and day of hire

    It is good practice to state within the contract the *day* as well as the date of the event. Sometimes a client has chosen a date for their event for a particular reason, such as a company anniversary, without realising the date falls on a Sunday, for example.

    Most corporate clients avoid Fridays for events because it is considered the start of the weekend. Likewise, weekend events are avoided because it is considered bad etiquette for a company to expect its staff or clients to be available at a weekend when this is 'family' time.

    If it is a family event provided by a company, such as a corporate fun day for clients or employees and their families, it could take place on a weekend.

    Celebrity-attended events tend to avoid Fridays and weekends because there is a general view that celebrities are unavailable or are away and out of the city.

- Hire period

    The hire period goes further than the date because not all hire periods are midnight-to-midnight or 24-hour hires.

    The contracted hire period states the start and finish times of the period of hire, which is not the same as when the doors open and close for the event.

    The hire period start time would usually be earlier than the beginning of the event itself because there will always be a need for deliveries and setting-up. This is known as the *get-in* time where the period of hire of the venue begins earlier than the event itself. So, the contracted hire period should commence with the required or allowed access or get-in time.

    Some venues are open to the public, so the venue should show the allowable access time. If the venue closes to the public at 6pm, say, the venue may not be accessible until all public have vacated the premises, which could be 7 pm: 7 pm would be the contracted hire period commencement.

    Sometimes, the event set-up is complex and will require one, two or more days in advance of the event. This is particularly so with exhibition set-ups, filming, highly technical events, for set-building, and for large theme and decoration projects. In such cases the hire period within the contract must state the accessible set-up days and times.

    If the event is in the early morning, there will be a need to hire the venue for all or part of the day before for set-up and rehearsals.

At the other end of the event – the end of the contracted hire period – it would be unusual for the hire period to end when the guests leave and the doors close.

It can take time to clear (*de-rig*) an event to dismantle (*strike*) sets, staging, technical equipment, theming, decoration, branding, installations and furniture. The venue must allow for this even if the client does not stipulate the need. Some clients may not wish to pay for extended times to de-rig because they are already in the venue, so what can the venue do about it anyway? This can lead to arguments, which is a risk the venue must plan to avoid. Conflict after an event can sour what was a successful event and the client/venue relationship can falter at this late stage. This leads to damaged reputation and to the loss of future business and repeat business.

The end of the hire period is referred to as the *get-out* time and the venue should be clear by that time.

A typical contracted hire period may read thus:

Event Date: Thursday 14th May

Hire Period: 06:30 Get-in (access from)

    16:00 Doors open

    21:00 Doors close

    00:00 Get-out (venue clear)

Set-up and de-rig days either side of the event day itself are usually discounted by the venue. The industry standard is 50% of the usual hire fee. This does vary from venue to venue, however, and may be open to negotiation depending on factors such as overall spend, the profile of the event and charity status.

A venue should not permit access to the venue before the contracted get-in time. A venue can easily control this.

However, a venue cannot easily control event over-runs or a de-rig that takes longer than anticipated. For this reason, the venue may charge penalties for over-staying the contracted hire period.

The venue hire contract must state the penalties incurred in such situations. In practice, however, venues are lenient and flexible. No venue wishes to inflict penalty charges upon their clients because it sours the relationship and harms future potential business. Penalty clauses exist to either deter overruns, or speed them up should they occur.

- Itinerary

    It is good practice for the venue to include an outline itinerary within the hire contract. This will show at an early stage that the venue and client are working to the same timings, which is important for the hire period. It will also demonstrate to the client that the venue understands the nature of the event.

    A typical outline itinerary may read as follows:

    16:00   Get-in for setting-up

    18:00   Rehearsal

    19:00   Doors open

            20:00 Presentation

            20:30 Dinner

            22:00 Dancing

            24:00 End

    01:00   Get-out and venue clear

An *outline* itinerary suggests the schedule could change. At the early stage of confirmation and raising the contract, timings must be allowed to change. The basic timings, and especially the get-in and get-out times (the contracted hire period) would not normally change.

- Cost of hire (also known as *hire fee*, *venue fee* or *facility fee*) and penalty charges should be clearly stated within the contract

- Payment structure

    The payment structure should be clearly set out in a contract. Usually, venues require a deposit to confirm the booking and book the date. Without a deposit the venue would not consider a booking as being confirmed, so the date is still at risk of being sold to another client. Similarly, a client should not consider that a venue is securely holding the date for their event until they have paid the deposit to the venue.

    The deposit would usually be 50% of the hire fee, but in some cases it can be the entire hire fee as the deposit to secure the date and consider the booking as confirmed. The balance of the hire fee (i.e. the remaining 50%) could be paid in stages set out in the contract. Always, the hire fee must be settled in full before the date of the event. Venues will stipulate in the contract how far in advance of the event the hire fee must be settled in full.

The contract will state that if the full hire fee is not received by the venue in advance of the event, the venue will cancel the booking.

- Cancellation procedure and charges

    Because events do cancel, the deposit can be anything from 50% to 80%. Some venues require 100% at the time of confirming the booking and signing the contract.

    Venues need to enforce a cancellation procedure because the client is reserving the date, and the venue needs to optimise its business. If the event cancels for whatever reason, the date can be left unsold and cannot be resold in the future – thus, event space is a perishable item because it has a date of expiry after which it cannot be resold.

    Events are cancelled for a wide range of reasons and it can be on the side of the client or the venue. There are elements out of anyone's control that necessitate a cancellation, such as the illness or death of a performer (think of Michael Jackson, for example, who was confirmed and booked to play London); inclement weather; lack of interest from guests, which would impact attendance, or from ticket-buyers, which would impact sales as a revenue stream; health and safety issues not overcome; or the inability to gain licences and permissions for the event to go ahead.

    Having a cancellation procedure makes things clear for both parties. It would be unprofessional to argue at a later stage about who cancelled, why and when. And, it would be unfortunate and expensive to have to take the matter to court.

    Usually, a venue would present its cancellation charges as a sliding scale. For example:

    100% refundable if cancellation is received in excess of two months prior to the date of the event.

    50% refundable if cancellation is received between two months and one month prior to the date of the event.

    Non-refundable if cancellation is received within one month prior to the date of the event.

This type of cancellation structure reflects the probability of the venue reselling the date to another client. The closer the cancellation is to the event date, the less likely the venue will resell that date to another client.

- Areas of hire

    All areas of the venue that are included within the hire fee should be identified within the contract. This would include room names; the use of break-out rooms; foyers; courtyards; terraces, gardens, lawns and annexes.

Where rooms or spaces are provided without additional charge and considered within the hire package, such as dressing rooms, a production office, changing rooms, or storage rooms, they must be listed on the venue hire contract as without additional charge.

- Facilities and services

    If the venue is providing facilities and services *within* the hire fee these should be listed within the contract as being included. For example:

    Hire includes cloakroom, 1× sound technician, 1× light engineer, 2× security, 1× event manager.

    Facilities and services which are *additional* to the hire fee should be noted in attachments to the venue hire contract. For example:

Catering	400 guests @ £20.00 per person
Beverages	charged by consumption
Disco	£150.00
Dance floor	£80.00

If the client has declined facilities or services, or is bringing their own, these should be stated, also. For example:

Balloon nets not required.

Gift bags: client's own.

To manage expectations and prevent misinterpretations it can be worthwhile for the venue to list the staff-count in the facilities and services section of the venue hire contract. For example:

6× waiters, 3× cloakroom attendants, 5× bar staff, 4× security

It should be remembered that the purpose of a contract is to uphold the responsibilities of each party. So, if a venue has promised 6 waiters and this is stated in the contract, it must duly provide the 6 waiters. Thus, both parties are protected and expectations are not misinterpreted or unfulfilled.

- Force majeure

    This clause holds no party liable for failures arising due to causes beyond their reasonable control. For example:

    Power failure

    Internet service failure

Fire, flooding, storms, earthquakes

Civil unrest

Industrial action

Acts of terrorism

- Liability and indemnity

Because the venue hire contract is a legal document, the insurance, health and safety, and damage to property clauses must be stated.

The venue should make clients aware that their valuables, clothing, display materials and other items may not be the responsibility of the venue. This should be clearly set out in the venue hire contract.

- Confidentiality

Many clients require confidentiality from the venue, the venue's staff, and their contractors. This is particularly required where celebrities or VIPs are attending an event. Also at conferences where sensitive corporate information, strategies, statistics or sales information may be revealed.

A good venue manager will want photographs of all events at their venue for use with future venue marketing purposes and their client portfolio. Permission for this activity should be stated within the venue hire contract so the client can authorise the use of their brand identity or company name.

AUTHOR'S VOICE BOX

At the BRIT Awards all staff are informed not to approach any artist. If any staff member approaches a VIP, celebrity or artist they will be ejected from the event.

There must be no photos, recordings or videos taken onsite. There must be no photographs taken of passes and wristbands.

No social media posts may be made relating to 'performers, guest presenters, costumes, performance details or any other descriptive details … until after 10pm on the night of the event'.

Notices are posted at all staff entry points to remind them of these rules.

- Anticipated number of guests

  The venue should state in the venue hire contract the anticipated number of guests and the date when final numbers must be finalised by the client.

  At this early stage, it would be acceptable to state 'minimum 100 guests'; '100–125 guests'; or 'maximum 125 guests'. What is important is to set the understanding of how many guests are expected to attend the event.

  This is important for anticipated catering numbers (and the revenue from catering), anticipated revenue from drinks sales, adequate staffing levels (and cost to the venue thereof), and to ensure that the client is aware of the maximum legal capacity of the venue which they are booking.

- Catering

  If the menu has not been decided at the point of raising the venue hire contract, it should simply state 'menu to be decided.' The menu choice can be included later as an annexe to the venue hire contract.

  However, the cost of the menu may already have been agreed because the client would have a budget which would include catering for their guests. Alto, the venue would require to know from the outset the spend on catering to ascertain the revenue from this stream. If this is so, the catering cost should be stated within the venue hire contract, even where there is no menu.

  Note: Catering and other costs are charged outside the venue hire fee and would not form part of the deposit. This is especially so with catering and bar (food and beverage or F&B), because exact costs for these areas cannot be determined until guest numbers are finalised, which may even be after the event has taken place.

  In such instances where final numbers of catering will be counted after the event, a *minimum guaranteed number* will be required by the event caterer or venue chef, whereby the client guarantees a minimum number of guests requiring food at the event. This allows for the venue to anticipate the revenue from this stream. It also protects the client from a situation where the caterer does not provide enough meals. And, it protects the caterer from providing 100 meals, say, when only 80 guests attend and the client insists on paying only for the number of guests who attended.

  Once the venue hire contract has been raised, it is sent to the client for approval and signature. When it is returned, the date of the event can be **confirmed** in the venue calendar.

Chapter 18

Lead-in procedure

The 'lead-in' is the period between the venue receiving confirmation and the date of the event.

To clarify:

1   The Enquiry Stage is from when the enquiry is received, until the booking is confirmed.
2   The Lead-In is from when the booking is confirmed, until the date of the event.
3   Pre-event management is the planning which happens before the event, that is during the lead-in period.
4   Operational event management is the running of the event onsite on the day of the event.
5   Post-event management are the procedures to enact after the event, such as debriefing meetings and guest satisfaction evaluation.

The venue must make good use of the lead-in period. From the point where confirmation is received there is opportunity for planning the event and nurturing the client relationship.

It is common practice but poor venue management to let a booking sit in the diary once it has confirmed. This can happen when a venue manager is too focused on sales and treats each sale as a conquest – 'job done' – and moves on to securing the next sale. If this style of management is allowed to occur, the lead-in period gets wasted and this essential planning time is compromised. The venue will tend to pick up the logistics too close to the event and be forced into a reactive style rather than proactive planning ahead of the event.

Allowing a lead-in period to dissipate, simply creates a shorter lead-in.

Venues which have a poor management structure typically tend to jump from one event to the next, which leads to developing a reactive management style, rather than a proactive management style.

A venue needs to achieve focus on the delivery of service standards to their confirmed clients. This in turn will achieve greater satisfaction and better sales because of repeat business, word of mouth referrals and good reputation.

AUTHOR'S VOICE BOX

Whether I am in the role of venue manager, client or freelance event specialist, I always allow a minimum three-month lead-in. This has become my rule of self-discipline.

The lead-in period between receiving a confirmed event and the date of that event is essential for gathering information, planning the concept, researching, finding and securing suppliers, and negotiating prices.

I have found that short lead-ins result in limited choices, quick decisions and knee-jerk reactions. When this happens the lead-in leads me, rather than me having the ability to manage the lead-in. Mistakes are made when time is short.

Venues can reduce the lead-in if there are quick-turnaround events. These may be small functions; frequent repeat business of the same type, such as meetings; repeat business from the same client, such as a monthly meeting; or short-notice bookings, such as wakes.

Even so, venues should calculate the lead-in required for each type of event they host so that they do not compromise the time to plan and organise an event.

Short lead-ins are manageable, so long as the people involved with the event understand how to achieve it all within in the limited time-frame available.

From the moment a booking confirms with the venue and until the event takes place (the lead-in period) a bond must exist between venue manager and client. After all, they are both working towards reaching the same objective of delivering a successful event.

The duty of the venue manager is to lead this relationship, not expect it. It takes work; it takes leadership.

It can be easy for a venue to think that the client is in power and will lead the relationship because they are paying the bill for the event. But, not all clients are aware of this as a role of event planning. Some clients want to lead (even when they should not be leading) yet other clients expect the venue to lead them.

Actually, the venue has the power because it knows the venue better than the client (the venue is the 'real' event manager) and will possibly know more about event management than the client (this is determined during building the client relationship). Whichever way it is, the venue must control everything that happens within their venue, which includes controlling the client relationship. This is where client relations are forged.

AUTHOR'S VOICE BOX

Most venue managers do not make the effort to visit the client at their office. This is because it is always convenient for the client to come to the venue for the show-round and ongoing meetings. The venue is where the event will take place and the client will want to visit to meet the chef or caterer, decorators, and other suppliers during the planning stages.

As a venue manager, I would often search for a reason to visit my clients as soon as possible at *their* place of work. Usually, I would deliver the contract to them by hand if practicable and use this as the reason to get to their office.

While at their workplace, I would be looking whether their working environment is relaxed or formal; modern or old-fashioned; organised or in disarray... I would see whether they have photographs on their desk of their children or partner, dog or cat, and we can begin talking about these interests.

I found such insights to a client valuable in forging the client relationship as I could ascertain the culture and work ethic of both my client and their organisation.

During the lead-in period the venue manager must gather information about the event and build a profile of the client.

The venue manager is there to provide assistance, first and foremost. Thereafter, to provide the services that have been agreed and ensure that they are delivered.

If following the practice of the one-person management structure as laid out in Chapter 9, the venue manager should remain the *one* point of liaison between the venue and the client, and must collate information from the venue's departments and suppliers to provide to the client.

It is for the venue manager to arrange meetings with departments and suppliers, and be present at such meetings. Not to be included in any meeting between the client and a supplier or department would mean losing control of the planning of the event.

Even one absence from a meeting could suggest to the client that the venue manager is not needed for everything. This is dangerous because the client could begin the process of talking to that other party for that particular need and the venue manager will become excluded. It may also allow a relationship to develop between the client and that other party which could undermine the control of the venue manager and result in being sidelined.

If the client requires menus and menu costs, the venue manager will liaise with the chef or catering manager for such information, and duly provide the menus and costs to the client.

If a menu tasting is required, the venue manager will arrange this meeting and will attend the tasting with the client. It is yet another opportunity to reinforce the client relationship.

The objective of venue management is that by the date of the event all information has been gathered by the venue manager and an established working relationship with the client exists.

Chapter 19

Client file procedure

A client file is opened for each client once confirmation is received.

All information about the event and the client, which is being gathered by the venue manager during the lead-in, is placed in to the client file.

At the point of confirmation when a new client file is opened, it would already include the Enquiry Form (now removed from the Enquiry File), the confirmation letter and the venue hire contract.

Every activity that occurs; each decision which is made by the client; every report of meetings, such as at the show-round and menu tasting, is placed into the client file.

By the time the event occurs the client file will be filled with detailed information about what has happened from the start of the project.

The client file should be so detailed that if the venue manager is absent for whatever reason, any other member of the venue team could pick up a client file and know every aspect of that event. *This* is how comprehensive the client file must be. To put it another way: nothing should be left out of the client file.

Here follows a list of what typically could be contained in a Client File:

- enquiry form
- client contact details
- notes and observations about the client; the client's likes and dislikes
- proposal
- venue hire contract
- quotes and discounts
- budget
- contact reports from meetings
- menu choice and tasting notes
- details of suppliers and contractors for the event (or the client's suppliers and contractors for the event), what they are providing, the quantities, prices, delivery details
- invoices
- debriefing notes
- Final Report.

It should be noted that where client information is held on a database or electronic file, data protection regulations must be observed for legal compliance.

Chapter 20

Client relationship procedures

Even at the early stage of confirmation the client relationship is already establishing itself. This is evident because the venue manager would have conducted a number of telephone conversations with the client, hosted the show-round, discussed requirements such as catering and technical needs, and possibly held subsequent meetings at the venue to satisfy the client for them to make their decision before the contract is raised and the booking is confirmed.

The enquiry process is usually short and the confirmation is received early. This is because clients are keen to secure their choice of venue for the date of their event.

Also, not much else can move forward with the planning of an event without knowledge of which venue will be hosting the event.

So, the bulk of building the client relationship happens after confirmation has been received by the venue.

However, that is not a rule. Sometimes, the enquiry procedure continues for a longer duration and may involve a number of show-rounds with various interested parties. If it is a film crew, for example, the location scout may visit the venue; then the location manager; then the director of the film...

Or, if a client is considering a range of suitable venues and has a lengthy lead-in period, they might be in less of a hurry.

For a venue, it can become frustrating to receive a potential client over an extended period and have to be available every time they wish to view the venue – without any guarantee that the event will go ahead as a booking.

It could mean having to prepare their ongoing demands such as costs, permissions and menus.

If the event does not confirm, it can feel like a bitter blow and not worth the effort. This could negatively impact the venue manager's future approach to demanding enquiries. But, every enquiry and each show-round is an opportunity to exercise the venue's enquiry procedures, as well as developing the venue manager's social skills and responses to questions.

The business of winning clients and hosting their events is largely about networking and contacts.

It must be kept in mind, therefore, that the people viewing a venue are still potential clients, even if this current event does not convert: these people will have future projects; they may move on to other companies; they will probably remain in the area of events and booking venues.

Additionally, each person is a potential referral to other people they know.

So, those people whom are considering the venue are an extension of the venue's public relations and marketing campaigns.

Once a booking is confirmed, the real work of building the client relationship begins. It should be remembered that relationships can deteriorate as well as strengthen. Experience teaches that if there is a long gap in communication, the relationship suffers from neglect.

Even if the confirmed event is straightforward for the venue, it is worthwhile for the venue manager to place courtesy calls to the client with the objective of maintaining the client relationship.

Complacency is an enemy. So, even if an event *is* straightforward (for the venue at least) – perhaps because it is a repeat of a previous event: a wedding at a wedding venue, for example, or a conference at a conference venue; or because it is a repeat client and their event is a reoccurrence – it must be treated such that each event is a new project and every client is an individual. Whatever the situation, any client deserves total support from the venue they have booked and are paying for.

It cannot be overstated how important is the venue-to-client relationship. For this reason, the one-person management structure (see Chapter 9) has been developed to ensure that the client is not passed from one person to another at the venue. If this happens, the client will need to rebuild relations from scratch with each new contact they encounter.

Importantly, if problems or challenges do occur, a good working relationship allows people to find solutions.

Chapter 21

Event schedule/ function sheet (Appendix III)

The event schedule (or *function sheet*) is an itinerary or 'running order' for the day of the event. Its purpose is to show everything which has been planned to occur onsite.

From start to finish – get-in to get-out – every action and responsibility is set onto the event schedule.

By the time the lead-in period finishes because the day of the event has arrived, every requirement for the event will be in place and set out on the event schedule.

If something is not on the event schedule, it has not been planned to happen. If it has not been planned to happen it should not be happening.

Nothing should happen in the venue if it is not known about and has not been planned. It is the venue manager's responsibility to know this; to understand this.

If a client should introduce an element on the day, the venue manager should consider refusing the request. No surprises must happen.

In events, surprise = risk.

The venue manager will begin constructing the event schedule as soon as the booking is confirmed. Thereafter, it is a working, organic, evolving document which gets continually updated so that no detail is left off the Schedule.

164   EVENT PROCEDURES FOR VENUES

Each time an action to happen at the event is known – is planned for – the venue manager will add it to the event schedule, until the exact itinerary for the event is finalised.

Close to the event day – one or two days prior, say – the event schedule is finalised and distributed to each person whom holds any responsibility at the event. Typically for a venue, it is distributed to each head of department so that every department is prepared for every event.

In many cases, the client might produce the event schedule – particularly if the client is an events organiser or an events company. In such situations, the venue manager must approve all activities within the Schedule before it is finalised and distributed. Usually, the venue manager would know what has been planned, but should be included with the approval of the event schedule, nonetheless.

Where the client *is* producing the event schedule, the venue manager may still produce a Schedule for the venue, heads of department and venue staff. This Schedule would be specific for the venue's requirements and would follow the format recognised by all members of venue management and staff. A copy of this schedule may be sent to the client for information because it may help confirm the alignment of expectations, but not necessarily so, as it is considered an internal document.

Although the event schedule is a document to show the itinerary on the *day* of an event, some events run for more than one day.

In some cases there will be activities occurring at the venue before or after the event date itself.

Before an event, there could be set-up day(s), stage-build days, décor and theme days, technical set-up, pre-event deliveries, or pre-event rehearsals. After an event it can be de-rig day(s) and collections.

In such cases, the event schedule will have one page for each day where some activity or responsibility occurs.

If the event itself runs for more than one day – such as a three-day exhibition – the event schedule should have one page for each day, even if one day is a duplication of the previous day. This is because, in most cases, there are minor adjustments to be shown for each day. The first day requires setting-up and the last day requires breaking-down, for example. But, there may be a party on the middle day, or an award to present on the final day, or a closing speech. These variants are important for the venue team to know.

EVENT SCHEDULE/FUNCTION SHEET

Appendix III provides an example of a function sheet/event schedule. However, the main points to include are as follows.

- Event title, date and short brief

    With venues which are busy with events it is necessary to include the event title, date and a short brief. This will prevent any confusion by staff or HODs who pick up the wrong event schedule. This is often a problem with staff noticeboards, where staff are looking at a similar but out-of-date event schedule.

    Even with venues which host infrequent events, mistakes can still happen if the event schedule does not show the title, date and a brief. So, it is good practice to do so.

    The event 'title' can be the client's name, company name, or type of event.

    The 'brief' will be a short description to explain the nature of the event to anyone reading the event schedule. It sets the context for the event and is important for temporary and casual staff so that they understand and appreciate the nature of the event. For example: *'This event is the product launch of a new fruity soft drink by Schweppes being promoted to drinks buyers, publicans, and the drinks industry press.'*

> **AUTHOR'S VOICE BOX**
>
> Some venue managers include a contact list on the front of the event schedule, which contains the names and telephone numbers of key personnel involved with the event.
>
> I do not like to include a contact list on an event schedule for two reasons.
>
> First, the names and telephone numbers of key personnel is sensitive information. The event schedule is a document which is copied and distributed to a range of personnel, staff, suppliers and providers, and often gets lost or left behind after an event.
>
> Second, I keep the contact details of key personnel in the client file, which never leaves me. So, if I need anybody's contact details, it is always to hand. I fail to see why everyone else needs such information.
>
> In venues there will be an office where names and phone numbers can be securely stored and easily retrieved, so it is senseless to include such information on an event schedule.

- Day and time

    The first column on the event schedule lists the time of an activity. The second column lists each activity. The third column lists who is responsible for the activity. The fourth column acts as a tick-list for the venue manager to check each activity has happened – thus, the event schedule becomes the venue manager's onsite checklist.

    | 16:00 | Rehearsal | Technical crew | ✓ |
    | 17:15 | Final walk-round | Venue manager | ✓ |

    It may be written to show the allowable timings of each activity.

    | 16:30–17:00 | Rehearsal | Technical crew | ✓ |
    | 17:15–17:20 | Final walk-round | Venue manager | ✓ |

- Distribution

    At the bottom of the Event Schedule there is a distribution list to show who should receive the document.

    This can be utilised by an email distribution group, but is an important tool to remind the events manager who requires a copy.

    It can be useful to mark each name on the distribution list when it is handed to the relevant recipient to identify who has lost their copy if it is found in the venue before or during the event.

Chapter 22

Operational procedures

Operational procedures are those which occur on the day of the event – the onsite procedures or *onsite logistics*.

The venue manager must act like the concierge of an excellent hotel: knowing from where to source all needs. The client may not be local, and in any case may not be experienced in managing events, whereas the venue manager has these two important advantages.

Because the planning of the event would have been undertaken during the lead-in period, every aspect which is to occur on the day of the event is anticipated and expected. Therefore, the main activity for the venue manager on the day of an event, is **checking**.

On the day of the event, the preparation duties of the venue manager are as follows.

- To ensure that the venue is accessible and ready to receive deliveries and the set-up crew.
- To ensure that the venue is ready to receive the client.
- To ensure that all services and facilities promised and detailed in the venue hire contract are delivered and available.

168 EVENT PROCEDURES FOR VENUES

- To oversee the delivery of all services and facilities, including catering, staff, cleaning, security.
- To oversee and liaise with all suppliers, providers and contractors.
- To receive the client, and provide continued and ongoing support and guidance.
- To source and facilitate any last-minute needs.
- To ensure that fire, health and safety procedures are followed.
- To ensure that risk assessment actions are upheld.
- To oversee rehearsals (and ensure that a rehearsal happens*).
- To conduct the briefing meeting to all venue staff (and ensure that the briefing happens*).
- To conduct the final walk-round of the venue before giving permission for the doors to open (and ensure that the final walk-round happens*). This is to check that all areas are ready, but is also for safety and legal reasons. Fire doors must be unlocked; escape routes must be kept clear; emergency lighting must be visible and working; fire-fighting equipment must be in place; there should be no trip hazards, such as cables, or dark edges of stages and platforms.

*Note: Where a procedure is set in place it must always be followed. The venue manager is responsible to ensure that procedures do happen. On event days, time can often become compressed due to set-up delays or miscalculations as to how long things will take. When this happens and there is pressure to open the doors on time, it is tempting to forego the rehearsal, or the staff briefing, or the final walk-round – but these procedures are inserted for necessity and must never be foregone. The purpose of a rehearsal is for the technical crew to practise their cues and timings; the staff briefing is to inform the staff of key information; and the final walk-round is to ensure that the venue is ready and safe before guests enter. If delays mean the doors open late, so be it. It is better to open the doors late than to omit a necessary procedure which was deemed important to be on the event schedule. Safety and professionalism must not ever be compromised, not even due to time limitations.

Until the point of the doors opening, the venue manager is in the role of checking to ascertain all planned activities have happened.

Once the doors are open and the event is in progress the operational duties of the venue manager are as follows.

- To check throughout the duration of the event that all services and facilities are maintained to set standards.

- To 'float' to all areas of the venue to ascertain the success of each delivery or understand any issues which may occur.
- To continuously monitor the legal and safety responsibilities of the venue.
- To proactively engage with the client and ensure that their expectations are being met.
- Should the client be dissatisfied, the venue manager should rectify the issue or monitor the situation so as to deal with the outcome after the event.

It can be seen how the venue manager continues in the role of checking throughout the duration of the event.

Because a venue manager knows the workings of the venue, it can be easy to get involved with the labour of it – especially where help is needed, such as in the cloakroom or behind the bar.

But the role of management is holistic: it requires overview.

It would be acceptable to help out to alleviate a problem, but it is not appropriate to become a worker.

A venue manager should be in a position to draft assistance from one area of the venue to another; from one department to another so as to alleviate a problem. If the cloakroom requires another pair of hands for 15 minutes, a member of staff should be drafted in, but it is not the venue manager's role to work the cloakroom for 15 minutes.

It is important for a venue manager to remain available for all areas and oversee the running of an event. It requires continual checking to achieve an understanding of how the event is running. If a client should be dissatisfied, the situation must be addressed, and remedied where possible.

It may be that a client makes a complaint after their event has happened, which is why the venue manager must retain a clear understanding of what is happening during the event. This can only be achieved by continual checking and will allow the venue manager to foresee a complaint, respond to it, and know whether it is legitimate.

When the doors close and the event is finished, the venue manager enacts the post-event procedures (see Part III).

Nothing unplanned should occur in a venue during an event. This is why the venue manager must ensure that all procedures are followed and included. If a procedure is omitted (such as the rehearsal, staff briefing, or final walk-round) the risk of unknown occurrences is much greater.

> ### AUTHOR'S VOICE BOX
>
> I have often been asked *who* is responsible for an event.
>
> This can become confusing when there is a client *and* a venue manager *and* an events organiser all onsite on the day of an event.
>
> The answer is simple to understand: everybody working on the event is responsible for the success of that event.
>
> However, it is the venue event manager who carries the greatest burden of responsibility. They know what works in the venue and what does not. They possess relationships with suppliers, the staff and the security team. They possess the skills and knowledge of event management, which other involved parties may lack. And they are best placed to remedy problems quickly and effectively.
>
> It is teamwork. I have never organised an event on my own.
>
> The client makes decisions based on advice from the venue manager and the event organiser.
>
> The event organiser makes things happen.
>
> The venue manager ensures the protection of the venue and everyone within it.

Chapter **23**

Get-in and set-up procedure

On the day of the event, the venue manager will know from the event schedule what time the set-up begins.

It is important for the venue manager to know when the client will arrive onsite, and should be available to receive the client. If the one-person management structure is being observed, the client will expect the venue manager to be present.

Clients often arrive to the venue after the get-in because they are not always involved with the set-up. So, the venue's responsibilities could begin before the client arrives.

The venue manager may not be required for the early duties of get-in and set-up, and could delegate this to an assistant, the technical manager or a member of security. If this is so, it is still the responsibility of the venue manager to ensure that the venue is accessible and ready to receive the deliveries and/or set-up crew. The delegated person must have possession of the event schedule; must have access to the premises; and must be briefed in readiness to oversee the get-in.

The venue hire contract works both ways – for the venue *and* for the client. The get-in time as stated in the venue hire contract is legally binding. Aside from this there is professional expectation. It would be unacceptable, unprofessional, and a breach of contract for a delivery or set-up crew to arrive at a venue which is unready, untended or inaccessible at the get-in time. Nobody should be waiting for a get-in to a venue – unless the venue is open to the public and the get-in cannot commence until the public have vacated the premises, in which case there is a variable to overcome and the get-in will wait until the go-ahead is given by the venue manager.

If a get-in does not go ahead according to the venue hire contract, and the time calculated for the set-up is thus compromised, it could compress the time between set-up and door-opening. This is where the rehearsal, the staff briefing, or the final walk-round get squeezed and are in danger of being omitted. Or the doors will open late.

If the get-in is delayed, the event schedule will become obsolete from the outset. All timings thereafter will be askew. And, everybody working the event will know that there was an operational issue caused by poor venue management.

It is worthwhile to note here that if any in-situ elements are not required for the event and need to be removed from the venue before the event – furniture, low-hanging chandeliers, etc. – they need to be removed *before* the get-in. If the client has not paid for these elements, they should not be in the venue during the hire period.

Some venues may use the set-up time (after get-in) to remove items not required. This is acceptable when the set-up of an event is not complicated or extensive.

In any case, the logistics and timings of removing items from the venue would be discussed and agreed with the client prior to the date of the event.

It is also worth noting that some venues will charge for the removal of unrequired items. Perhaps they incur costs for removing light fittings or equipment requiring specialist technicians, or they have no storage capacity for unused tables and chairs and will incur costs for transportation, labour and temporary storage.

23.1 Set-up

If the venue manager is not required onsite for the get-in they will arrive at some point during the set-up. The time of arrival of the venue manager will be prearranged and shown on the event schedule.

The first role will be to **check** whether everything is on schedule at this early stage. Using the event schedule, the venue manager will check that the deliveries have arrived; check that the set-up crew are on schedule; check with the production or technical manager that all is well, so far.

Chapter 24

Rehearsal procedure

During set-up, the venue manager will check that the actual timeline is on schedule and will allow for the rehearsal. This is important to determine because rehearsals can get delayed or even cancelled if time runs out.

It is the duty of the venue manager to ensure that a rehearsal does take place because it is their venue on show and nothing would be worse than a failure on stage in full view of the guests. So, even where timings are out, the rehearsal must happen – even if this means the doors will open later than planned.

If there is a stage, there must be a rehearsal. And, whoever is on the stage must have rehearsed.

If there is a band or entertainment, the rehearsal will allow for sound checks so that the production crew can adjust sound levels and microphone levels.

The production crew will also set the lighting levels for the show and the lighting engineer will *'focus'* the lights to create pattern or *'gobo'* effects and illuminate particular spots.

Where presenters, speakers or presenters of awards are appearing at the event, each person must rehearse their slot. This allows for timing adjustments, lighting adjustments and sound adjustments. It also allows each presenter the surprise of hearing their own voice channelled through a sound system. Presenters should be shown how to hold and speak through a microphone. They should also be made aware of camera or photo angles, and where to access and leave the stage.

A rehearsal is not only for the benefit of people on the stage. It is an essential procedure for the production crew, stagehands, cameramen and backstage 'runners'.

The production manager will run through the sound and lighting cues so that the entire crew have at least one try-out before the show.

Where recipients of awards are not rehearsing – because they may not be at the venue before the event, or the winners are kept secret until they are announced – stand-ins play the role of the winners attending the stage to receive their awards. This allows the sound engineer, lighting engineer, follow-spot operators and camera crews to rehearse following each winner from their designated seat to the stage. In addition, rehearsing with stand-ins walking to and from the stage enables the production manager to accurately time the show.

Chapter 25

During-event procedures

Before the doors open for guests to enter the venue, the venue manager will conduct the staff briefing.

This briefing meeting should last for 5–10 minutes and no longer than 15 minutes, because staff will be busy preparing for guests to enter.

The main points to cover in a staff briefing are as follows:

- opening and closing times
- what the event is for
- introduction of key personnel – venue manager; client; head of security
- timings, such as when the entertainment will begin, what time dinner is served, when the bar will close
- the location of cloakroom and toilets, so that staff who are unfamiliar with the venue can direct guests to these areas when asked.

The staff are usually briefed as one group for efficiency and consistency, and not briefed in departmental groups. This allows for just one briefing, because time will be short. If any member of staff has a question, all other staff will hear the answer. Also, it prevents the venue manager from having to repeat information or forgetting to say something to one group which they have said to another. In addition, if there is a chance that staff will be utilised in other areas – a waiter being utilised to help out in the cloakroom, say – one briefing maintains consistency across the departments.

25.1 Security briefing

After the staff briefing, the venue manager may separately brief the security team. Security will need to know that the doors do not open until the venue manager gives the instruction; not the client nor the event organiser. It is imperative that the venue manager conducts the final walk-round, even if it means that the doors will open late. The client or the event organiser may not agree with this, but security will not open the doors until the venue manager gives approval.

Also, security need to be briefed about VIPs attending the event and different types of identification and access passes. Where areas are distinct – such as hospitality areas, VIP areas, backstage areas, crew areas – the security personnel stationed at these distinct areas must be briefed as to which passes allow access.

At each distinct area, a poster should be displayed with each type of pass visible (backstage; crew; artistes; VIP; guest; Access All Areas). There will be a cross through the passes which do not allow access to that area. (Access All Areas passes provide unlimited access to all areas of the venue, so will not be crossed out on any poster.)

This poster system avoids embarrassment and prevents conflict. The holder of the pass can clearly see where they are permitted to attend without having to ask security. It also prevents security from having to challenge or embarrass guests. And, the posters provide a visual support to security so they cannot be accused of making personal or wrong decisions.

Note: Access All Areas (or *Triple A* or *AAA*) passes allow access without restriction to every area of the venue. However, there may be further stipulation as to whether the holder of an Access All Areas pass can escort other parties into certain areas. For example, a person with an Access All Areas pass may escort somebody with a Hospitality pass to the backstage areas but not the crew areas.

25.2 Final walk-round

Before giving the instruction for doors to open, the venue manager will conduct the final walk-round. This is a brief but thorough walk around all areas of the venue. It is the final *check*.

Because the walk-round is the final check, it is the last of the preparation procedures. This means it happens as the last activity before doors open.

DURING-EVENT PROCEDURES

When the venue is ready and it is almost time to open the event to guests, this is when the venue manager instructs security to *hold the doors closed*. The venue manager will then conduct the final walk-round.

The final walk-round can be conducted by the venue manager alone, or with the accompaniment of the client, and/or the event organiser, and/or the head of security, and/or the head of housekeeping or maintenance. Being accompanied by any of these personnel may quicken the procedure if anything requires correcting as a result of the final check.

The purpose of the final walk-round is to *check* that all areas of the venue are ready and safe to receive guests.

- All areas are clean.
- No cleaning products have been left behind.
- No cleaner's rooms, maintenance rooms or storerooms have been left unlocked.
- Bars are set up and staff are ready.
- Cloakroom staff are ready.
- DJ/stage/entertainment is ready.
- Lighting and sound is in the correct mode to receive guests into the venue.
- Fire exits are unlocked and unchained.
- Emergency escape routes are not obstructed.
- Emergency lighting is not covered by decorations or branding.
- There are no trip hazards, such as cables, platform edges, legs of tripod stands.
- The front door is ready to receive guests and the door hosts are in place with guest lists.

If an issue is identified during the final walk-round, it must be remedied before the permission is given for security to open the doors. This would usually cause only minimal delay or perhaps no delay at all if the walk-round is ahead of schedule.

After an issue has been identified, the venue manager can continue with the walk-round but must always return to the issue to ensure that it has been rectified. It is easy for somebody to say they will rectify a problem, or to say they *have* taken care of it, but the venue manager must recheck before opening the doors. If it was worth checking in the first place, it has to be worth rechecking.

Only when the final walk-round is complete and the venue manager is satisfied, will permission be granted for security to open the doors.

178 EVENT PROCEDURES FOR VENUES

> **AUTHOR'S VOICE BOX**
>
> Clients will panic when they realise the doors are not going to open on time. They see it as some kind of failure. They will be horrified at the thought of their invited guests having to wait outside and not be welcomed into the venue on time.
>
> But, procedures are implemented for good reason and must be followed. In the case of the final walk-round it is for reasons of safety and risk. Nothing is more important: not even opening the doors on time.
>
> Many times after a hectic set-up and the lights having been dimmed into ready mode, I have conducted a final walk-round of the venue and come across broken glass; cables strewn across carpets; trip hazards; cleaning chemicals left behind; and cleaner's cupboards left open. I have even found fire exits still chained.
>
> On one occasion, I discovered a rusty metal fitting protruding from a wall.
>
> There are legal implications to consider, as well as safety, health, presentation standards and quality, which supersede the need to open the doors on time.
>
> It really is worth keeping guests waiting outside for a short while so as to ensure their safety once inside the venue.

25.3 Opening the doors

Opening the doors is the moment it has all been for – the doors are open and the venue is receiving guests.

All the preparation and liaison; client meetings; venue visits; all the planning ... it has come down to this point of opening the doors and allowing guests into the venue.

The point of entry is where the first problems can arise. The door is where the venue manager should take position.

The entrance can be an area of high activity with guest list, VIP list, press list, the press taking photos, door hosts, security checks, passes being checked, tickets or invitations being checked, guest drop-offs, guest arrivals, the cloakroom, and the service of welcome drinks (although hopefully not; see section 14.3.1).

At the door, the venue manager must *check* that guests are being welcomed politely and efficiently into the venue. The flow of guests must be monitored to ensure speed of service and that queues are not forming.

Once the venue manager feels confident the entrance is running smoothly, they can move to check other areas, but will continue returning to the front door to monitor this area until the flow of guests arriving at the venue subsides.

For the next checks, the venue manager can follow the natural flow of a guest entering the venue. The next area to check, then, would be the cloakroom.

Just like at the front door, it is necessary to monitor the flow of guests. If a queue is forming, it could be worthwhile to place additional staff into the cloakroom during the busy arrivals period, until the flow of guests slows down.

The venue manager can leave the front areas to now check how the welcome drinks service or bars are operating. Once satisfied that these areas are operating well, there should be a return visit to the cloakroom and front door.

25.4 Checking

Once arrivals have slowed, the critical period for the front door, cloakroom and welcome drinks has passed.

Now, the venue manager can leave these areas and move into the venue to monitor the event.

Using the event schedule as a checklist, each activity can be checked as it is scheduled to occur.

The venue manager should work ahead of the schedule, so as to remain proactive. If there is a show, speech or presentation, the venue manager will liaise with the production manager before the show is scheduled to begin.

Ongoing checking of timings and making necessary adjustments is helpful. It may be that dinner service is running late, so the show will begin later than scheduled. This can be communicated to the production manager.

Delays and adjusted timings are common with events; it is part of the nature of events. The venue manager should be aware of timing variances by using the event schedule and measuring how askew the timings are.

Timing adjustments need to be communicated to the team: the chef; the production manager; the presenter, speaker, host or entertainment; and maybe the client.

Where timings do change as the event is progressing, it is good practice to make notes on the event schedule. This way the venue manager has a record of when activities actually occurred against the planned timing. If the canapé service is late, for example, it will be recorded as such. This information will provide a reminder after the event and may help if a complaint is raised.

It should be that during the event, the venue manager is checking and monitoring all operations within the venue: toilets, bars, catering, technical production, cloakroom, security …

Additionally, the venue manager should frequently meet the client to *check* that expectations are being met. Mere eye contact may be enough. Or observing from a distance that the client appears to be enjoying the event. If done correctly, the venue manager will be visible to the client in case anything is required, but can move on if all is well.

It is courteous and respectful to demonstrate attentiveness to the client. They hold the purse; they make the decision whether to rebook; they enjoy being looked after; and all clients have an ego to be massaged.

The checking procedure is a professional tool to ensure that an event is running as had been planned during the lead-in stage. However, it is also the event manager's tool should things not go to plan.

Notes and timing variances should be made on the event schedule for recollection after the event.

At the end of the event, the right-hand tick-column on the event schedule should be filled, without gaps, to confirm that every activity had indeed occurred and was checked.

25.5 Catering

Regardless of whether serving a buffet, a banquet, or straightforward canapés, the catering can be a cause for complaint at events.

It may be a guest or number of guests who complain, or it might be the client who was dissatisfied.

Everybody knows their idea of good food, so everybody has their opinion.

The problem is that poor catering, or a complaint about catering, harms the reputation of the venue. Remember, the venue manager must protect the reputation of the venue. Yet, catering is the easiest and possibly most common cause of damage to a venue's reputation.

For this reason, the venue manager must feel confident that the food quality is high. This confidence is provided at the early stages of planning the event because it will either be in-house catering or external. If it is external (an outside caterer or event caterer), the venue manager would have recommended which caterer the client could use from the approved list. If there was not an approved list and the client brings in an unknown caterer, the venue manager would have met with the caterer, liaised with them, and sampled their food at a menu tasting.

So, by the date of the event, the quality of catering would be known.

During the event, the venue manager must ensure that catering standards are upheld by closely checking and monitoring as part of the onsite management procedures. Carrying out this procedure diligently should have forewarned the venue manager of any issues with the catering.

If a complaint arises, the venue manager will thus be prepared to receive it, and may even have already arrived at a solution.

No less important, is for the venue manager to know whether a complaint is legitimate.

It has been known for clients to 'invent' complaints as a tactic to negotiate the final invoice. If the venue manager has performed the role of checking every area during the event, and is armed with notes and timing variances on the event schedule, complaints can be countered and seen as legitimate (see Section 27.3).

25.6 Closing

There is often a natural 'wind down' of an event. This could be determined by slowing the pace and style of the music, the end of the band's set, the closure of the bar, or the natural drift of guests exiting the venue.

Towards the end of an event, the venue manager's focus should revert to the cloakroom and front door. These areas will again become busy and it really is very easy to predict.

At the start of an event, and at the end, guests will want easy entering, easy exiting and easy access to the cloakroom. It is a failure of venue management to get this wrong.

The venue manager's role does not finish at the end of an event. It continues past the end of the event. So, what is determined as the 'end'?

The 'end' is not when the catering has finished. Nor is it when the client leaves the venue. Nor is it when the last guest has gone home.

The job of a venue manager continues through the de-rig and to the get-out. It should be noted and understood that a de-rig can be one of the most risk-prone parts of an event (see Chapter 26), and venue responsibility only ends when the venue is clear.

Only when the venue is clear, does the venue manager come to the end. But, then the post-event procedures kick in.

Venue management is a social role in a social environment, which requires a venue manager to be a social person. The client relationship depends on it. But, the *job* is not to be social. The job is to be professional and attentive; to guide and lead; to perform the function of a manager; to take control of situations that may occur; to remain aware of hazards; to manage people. To be sober.

> **AUTHOR'S VOICE BOX**
>
> It is not the job of a venue manager to be sipping cocktails with the client – even if the 'end' of the event is determined as something other, such as after the show, and the client is feeling more relaxed.
>
> A venue manager is at work and is in a position of responsibility and authority.
>
> It is acceptable to sip a cocktail or a glass of champagne with the client to be sociable. But I take the drink with me and discreetly deposit it elsewhere.
>
> If anybody were to follow me around at an event, they would find behind me a trail of glasses with just one sip taken from each!

Event guests can be unpredictable, especially as the event wears on. They are in an unfamiliar environment and surrounded by temporary installations. Almost all events contain alcohol, which increases the risks. This book has already identified how guests are not aware of safety and treat their personal safety with complacency – they are having a good time. Somebody is required to oversee safety and behaviour, and it should be the venue manager who takes this role. People are relying on it.

The job of a venue manager is to minimise or eliminate all risk. This cannot be achieved to the highest possible degree if the venue manager is part of the risk.

Chapter 26

De-rig procedure

The de-rig occurs at the end of an event, which is why a venue manager must remain attentive – and sober – throughout the event. The de-rig is no less another part of an event and, as such, has to be managed.

In addition, de-rigs are often hazardous, with equipment being dismantled as quickly as possible because the crew have finished the event and just want to get home.

Crew are careful with a get-in and set-up because elements required for the event have yet to be used and are about to be on view to guests. The de-rig, however, comes after elements have been used and guests have departed. The same care does not apply at this end of the event. Often, most elements will not be used again and get torn down quickly and frenetically.

Much attention to safety must be devoted to all parts of the event, including the hazard-filled de-rig.

The de-rig – that is the breaking-down of an event – should not ever commence until after all guests have exited the venue. The venue manager must not allow a client, event organiser or technical crew to commence the de-rig before all guests have left.

De-rigs are usually noisy and messy (and crew can be noisy and messy, also). The stage backdrop gets ripped down, the chairs get stacked, the technical crews strip their equipment from the venue... These are not activities which guests should witness after the care and expense that was spent on the aesthetics of the event.

A de-rig is a 'backstage' activity, and backstage areas are out of sight to guests.

> ### AUTHOR'S VOICE BOX
>
> I never allow the venue to begin a de-rig while guests remain in the venue.
>
> Often, a venue will begin stacking chairs or whipping off cloths from tables because they sense the end of the event and are over-keen to clear up the place and send the staff home. I find this wholly unprofessional after the work and expense we all put in to dressing an event and making it a wonderful experiential experience for our guests to enjoy.
>
> If there are guests still onsite, I will stop a venue from fraying the edges of my event and exposing what lies beneath.

Only in the situation of a 'turn-around' does a de-rig commence while guests are in the venue. A turn-around occurs when a room is used for dual purposes and is changed into another format so that the event can continue.

For example: after a conference, the conference room can be *turned-around* to become the dinner venue for delegates. Usually, the turn-around occurs while the guests are absent – while they are changing for dinner, for example.

Often, wedding venues need to turn-around their space because room is limited. So, after the wedding breakfast, guests will be asked to vacate to the gardens or the bar. Then, some tables will be cleared from the dancefloor and the DJ will set up. Then the guests can return for the celebration party.

PART III

Post-event procedures

Chapter 27

Post-event procedures

The period after an event has taken place is where the loose ends are tied up and any remaining invoices are settled. Some event organisers call this stage the *'wash-up'*.

What is important is the legacy of each event.

The reputation of the venue is largely measured after an event. So if the post-event procedures are left untidy or neglected, this will be the legacy.

It must be remembered that the events industry is cyclical. Relationships matter because they revisit. Every client is a potential repeat client. Suppliers may be needed again for a future project. Reputations carry through the industry and people do speak to each other. If the after-event procedures and follow-ups, such as paying final invoices, are not followed through efficiently, this is how the venue will be remembered.

It can take effort to continue with procedures after an event has taken place. This is because of the anti-climax. Often, the client will move onto other things at their workplace now that the event is behind them, and it will be tiresome for the venue manager to chase the client to push on with completing the last procedures.

188 POST-EVENT PROCEDURES

For a venue, there may be the next event project and client on which to focus.

But, all procedures are purposeful, so a venue manager cannot omit any part. Each procedure makes up the whole: the 'whole' is the success of an event and is only complete when the three stages of event management have been fulfilled.

1. Pre-event: the lead-in, which is the planning stage from the point of receiving confirmation to the date of the event.
2. Onsite: the operational logistics on the day of the event.
3. Post-event: the follow-up and evaluation after the event.

It would be neglectful to omit the post-event requirements from the three stages of ensuring the success of an event. Success can only be measured after the event.

The post-event stage is the time to measure performance. This is when it can be ascertained whether the objectives of the event were met; whether the client was satisfied; whether there were any issues that affected the venue or departments within the venue; whether the guests enjoyed the experience; what were the learnings for future events; and how good a job was done.

The post-event stage is the learning for the next event.

The way to gauge the success of an event is not only by the event itself. It would be folly to ask guests leaving an event if the event was a success – they would not know what the measurements are.

Asking guests is not a reliable measurement of success – guests will usually wish to be polite in their response when asked if they had a good time. If alcohol was a component of the event, guests will be buoyed by drink, which makes this an even less reliable strategy for measuring success.

Guests may state that they enjoyed themselves and had a good time, but this could be only one objective of the client when deciding to stage an event and putting a budget to it. Was the client's purpose only for guests to have a good time? Or were the client's objectives for the event – the *reasons* for it – also to make money; or to raise funds for a charitable cause; or to promote a product; or to launch a product; or to raise their company profile; or to communicate a message … ?

Event objectives are set at the beginning of an event, so the venue manager must understand the reasons that the client is choosing to stage the event and putting a budget to it. Only after the event, can it be seen whether those objectives were met.

It is polite and courteous to ask guests whether they had a good time as they leave the venue. It will also provide a modicum of understanding whether the objective of providing guests with a good experience was largely achieved. But, there are other strategies to employ which will produce more reliable and structured results.

27.1 Debriefs

After the event has happened, the venue manager should hold meetings to reflect on the event.

The venue manager will treat debriefs not as the 'closing chapter' of an event, but the beginning of the preparations for this client's next event, should there be one (and there is always potential for a repeat booking).

Debriefs provide the venue manager with a further sales opportunity. And, if something *did* go wrong with the last event, the debrief is the procedure which can lead to the recovery.

27.1.1 Venue debrief

After each event, the venue manager should hold a debriefing meeting with the heads of department to ascertain their views about the smooth running of the event.

If the event was routine, the venue debrief may be swift. It may even be tempting to forego this debrief after a few events have happened at the venue. But this is another procedure which makes up the 'whole' of creating a successful event, so a debrief must happen every time.

However routine an event may seem, there might always be something different or which happened differently. Each client will be different, for sure. So it is good practice to sit down with the heads of department and obtain their insights as to the success of an event.

The real purpose of the venue debrief is to identify problem areas and learn from them so that they are not repeated. This is the learning.

If a department reports an issue, the procedures can be adapted for future events, and the venue manager needs to evolve this learning for the sake of self-development, professionalism, the success of future events, and the ongoing reputation of the venue.

Also, venue debriefs provide a forum for the venue manager to be made aware of any issue that arose during an event so that it is known before the client raises it during the client debrief (see section 27.1.2). This is why the venue debrief happens before the client debrief.

27.1.2 Client debrief

The purpose of the client debrief meeting is to ascertain and ensure that the client was satisfied and their expectations were met. A venue manager will also wish to know that the event objectives were met.

The level of client satisfaction may already be known to a certain extent because the venue manager would have been liaising with the client during the event. Sometimes, however, a client will appear to be enjoying themselves because it may not be appropriate to raise an issue during the event, or they do not wish to be seen to be making a fuss.

The venue manager would usually receive some feedback from the client as they leave the venue, or by phone or email the day after the event.

The venue manager should therefore possess a reasonable idea of the client's level of satisfaction with the event.

Even so, it is necessary to ensure that the client debrief does happen for deeper and more structured feedback after a short period of reflection. The client debrief also helps to continue the client relationship, so that it does not cease at the end of the event. Furthermore, this debrief provides a sales opportunity for repeat business.

This meeting allows the client relationship to be extended past the event and towards any possible event in the future.

Any opportunity to extend the client relationship and win repeat business or referral business should be sought, and the client debriefing meeting is the most obvious means.

If the event was successful, the client debrief meeting will be cordial and relaxed. If there was an issue, the meeting will provide a conduit to discuss and settle the matter.

This is why the client debrief should be pre-scheduled: it is not enough to adopt the attitude that 'everything went well' so a meeting is not needed. Or, there was an issue which 'I do not want to deal with'. If the meeting is already in the diary, it will happen.

If there was an issue during the event, of which the venue manager is unaware, the client debrief meeting provides the opportunity for the client to discuss it with the venue manager directly, rather than complain to other parties.

If the venue manager is already aware of an issue because it was identified during the checking procedures at the event, or an issue was raised at the venue debrief with the heads of department, a solution can be found before the client debrief happens.

If a client complains after an event and the issue was not known about via the checking procedures or the venue debrief, the complaint may not be legitimate. This is why the venue debrief happens first, and why the onsite checking procedures are crucial. The venue manager should be cautious if, after all these procedures, a client raises a new issue that has not already been identified.

It may be that guests have raised an issue to the client and the venue manager would not know this.

But it might be that the client is creating an issue or exaggerating it as leverage against outstanding invoices. There are ways of dealing with client complaints, which are set out in Section 27.3.

The client debriefing should be considered as a social interaction to close the event. The meeting has its purpose and objectives, but should come across to the client as a gesture of hospitality.

It can take place at the venue or at the client's office, which would possibly be more formal. Or it could take place in a social environment, such as a restaurant, which would help with discussing potential future business.

All debrief meetings should be scheduled on the event schedule so that the heads of department and the client anticipate them happening and can prepare for them. It also helps with diary planning.

If debriefs are not pre-scheduled, there is a risk they may get omitted after the event has happened and everybody has moved on to other projects.

The venue debrief would happen the day after an event; the client debrief should happen within one week of the event.

27.2 Guest satisfaction evaluation

Events have many objectives and reasons for happening. Whatever the objectives and reasons, all events are for entertaining people. Every event has the objective for guests to have a good experience – even if the event is for a serious cause.

A client will want to know whether their event was judged a success by the people who attended.

A venue needs to know that people enjoyed themselves and had the best possible experience at the venue.

Such feedback is essential for improving and evolving facilities, services and procedures. This measurement and understanding is how venues grow success.

It is always valuable to evaluate guest satisfaction.

It has become common practice to email a short questionnaire either to all attendees or a sample proportion of them.

So, even when guests appear all smiles as they leave the event, and if the door staff report that every guest left happy, a questionnaire is still necessary to obtain opinions which are reflective and structured.

Besides, a questionnaire allows for specific questions to be asked and for the guest to reply in a considered manner. And, it would not be appropriate nor acceptable to delay a guest by asking questions as they are leaving an event.

A post-event questionnaire should be sent to guests the day after the event. This is necessary so as to obtain honest feedback while the event is fresh in the mind of the guest. Also, it is important to have received the feedback and analyse the results before the client debrief meeting.

The questions asked within a questionnaire depend upon the information required by the client, venue and sometimes the event organiser. No more than ten questions is deemed appropriate because a questionnaire must be quick to complete. If a questionnaire is longer there will be fewer responses, because people have had the experience of the event and cannot be bothered with a lengthy questionnaire afterwards.

Ideally, the guest feedback questionnaire would be designed prior to the event and will have been circulated to the other management parties for their input. It may be that one manager wishes to insert questions pertinent to their area of responsibility – the chef may wish to insert question about the food, perhaps.

The questionnaire should reflect the objectives of the event, so that by the time the feedback is received, it provides the measure of whether the objectives were in fact met.

Preparing the questions in advance ensures that this procedure is not forgotten or omitted after the event. It also allows for consideration of what to ask on the questionnaire and which guests will receive it.

Questions to consider for a guest feedback questionnaire may include the following.

- Did you have difficulty finding the venue?
- Do you think the venue was suitable for this event? Why/why not?
- Do you feel that the staff were friendly and helpful?
- Did you have to queue at the cloakroom/toilets/bar/buffet?
- How do you rate the quality of food?
- Please name three sponsors that you saw represented at the event.
- Please name three brands that you saw represented at the event.
- Did you enjoy the entertainment?
- What time did you leave the event?
- Would you attend this event again?
- Would you attend this venue again?
- Did you find the event to be good value for money?
- What did you most enjoy at the event?
- What did you least enjoy at the event?
- What other comments would you like to make regarding your experience at this event?

The questionnaire may also be used as a sales tool – such as the question asking whether the guest would attend this event again. If the response is 'yes', then an invitation or booking form can be sent out for next year's event.

In many cases, a client will want to send the questionnaire themselves because they are likely to possess the contact details of attendees. Remember, the questionnaire must be sent according to 'confirmed arrivals'. It would not be professional to send a questionnaire to guests who did not attend the event, even if they had said they would attend.

If the client wants control over the questionnaire, the venue manager will need to ask for a few questions to be inserted which directly relate to the performance of the venue.

All post-event procedures should be completed quickly and with a sense of urgency. Otherwise, complacency sets in and it will take yet greater effort for other parties to assist with these procedures.

27.3 Problem solving

The one key to solving problems is communication.

Poor communication exacerbates difficult situations.

It is not good management to ignore an issue or avoid a client's phone calls and emails. Face to face communication is always the best way to resolve problems – and if the client briefing has been pre-scheduled it encourages face-to-face problem solving.

Even where a client briefing is not scheduled, a problem provides the reason to now arrange a client debrief meeting to discuss a solution.

The potential here is to identify the issue, work towards a solution, and recover the client relationship.

It should be kept in mind that the reputation of a venue is paramount. Venues must protect their reputation. This requires past clients to be loyal and speak favourably. Avoiding a problem is the easiest way to wreck a reputation: the opportunity is to work together with the client towards a resolution.

Referrals and repeat business are essential to the success of a venue. This is where the pre-scheduled client debrief becomes valuable.

If there are no issues after the event it is a social follow-up meeting.

If there happens to be an issue it forces the two parties together to seek a solution.

Either way, the client debrief provides a channel of communication and dialogue. Where there is a problem, communication and dialogue is the only way forward. It is all about recovering that vital client relationship.

When emotions and prejudices are put aside, solutions become visible.

POST-EVENT PROCEDURES

> **AUTHOR'S VOICE BOX**
>
> Any of my clients who felt they had an issue with their event were those clients who became my repeat clients or long-standing friends.
>
> This was down to the extra effort needed for me to resolve a situation and avoid conflict. Protecting or recovering the client relationship is always the goal.
>
> After all the hard work that goes into planning an event, and the dealings with the client, and the physical effort onsite at the event itself, it would be tragic to fall at the last hurdle by not maintaining the client relationship after the event has happened.
>
> This is where the client debrief has proved so valuable – I wouldn't end an event without it.

The best form of defence is the tenacity of liaising, checking and monitoring during the event. A venue manager must feel confident – and be honest about it – that everything which occurred during the event was planned and was executed to the highest standard.

Even where standards fall short – perhaps through no fault of the venue – the venue manager will know about it through the onsite checking procedures.

It has already been noted in this book that some clients may 'create' issues before settling the final invoices. For this reason, many venues insist there are no outstanding payments before the event takes place. This is a protection mechanism, but it does not rule out complaints and arguments.

In any situation, the venue manager needs to be aware of the good and bad of an event.

It is easier to find solutions if the complaint is legitimate – not because the solutions are easier, but because otherwise mistrust enters the equation. Mistrust causes emotional barriers. But, whether a complaint is legitimate or not, the venue manager must resolve the situation and recover the client relationship.

Solutions begin with dialogue. It is important to understand the client's point of view. It is also helpful to ascertain what the client would like to compensate for the issue.

196 POST-EVENT PROCEDURES

A venue manager should not use blame as a reason for falling short of expectations. It can be easy to blame other departments, suppliers, attendees, or even the client. Blame does not resolve an issue. Rather, it exacerbates an issue by causing conflict and defensiveness.

After blame, the next way of dealing with a complaint will be to offer discounts to compensate the client. Remember, this could be what the client is searching for.

A discount from the invoice can placate a client, but it will not resolve an issue – and it will impact on profit to the venue. So, discounts are a way of keeping the client quiet without providing a real solution.

The venue could waive the bill and provide a facility or service for free – complimentary, or *'comping'* the bill. Like discounting, it pacifies a client but does not provide a solution. It will also impact on profit to the venue.

If a venue discounts or comps its services on a regular basis, it risks creating the reputation of poor service because it is not working to find solutions to resolve its issues. The issues are still present and are likely to be repeated. Venues which routinely discount and comp because of complaints are those that rarely reflect on how to improve their service.

Once word spreads that this venue is cheaper if a complaint is lodged, clients may take the opportunity to invent issues in the certain knowledge they will receive a discount or get the bill waived. Perhaps the venue will receive business from clients for this very reason.

This form of problem solving is not sustainable. Eventually, the reputation will be harmed, the quality of clients will deteriorate, staff morale will decline, profit margins will be compromised and the business will close.

It is a solution to offer a discount or comp for a client's next event, rather than doing so for an event which has already happened and there is no opportunity to correct it.

This way, the venue provides itself with the opportunity to put things right and demonstrate how wonderful things can be, while the client receives the solution they were looking for (only it is in advance).

The venue manager will need to assure the client that they will receive exemplary standards and service next time – so long as this can be delivered. Usually, a venue will take note of what went wrong and then go to extra effort to ensure that the second experience surpasses the first.

Clients who do respond to discounts or comps can be swayed to receive this benefit in advance of their next event. It is an incentive to return to a venue and receive an exceptional service for a lesser budget.

If the client relationship procedures discussed in this book have been followed, a client will provide the venue manager with the benefit of belief that their next event will be excellent. And it must be.

Just because a rebooking is discounted, the venue must not compromise its commitment of facilities and services, even if it does impact on profit margins. The venue must remember why the discount was offered in the first place.

Sometimes, a venue will take a booking which has a restricted budget or they will agree to take a booking as a corporate or personal favour. Even so, the venue took the choice to accept the booking and must not provide a 'discounted service' to the client. It is not fair to the client and is harmful to the reputation of the venue: would the guests know that this was a discounted booking?

A venue's commitment to exemplary standards of service and professionalism must never fall short.

When a client rebooks a venue, procedures must already have been tightened so that a negative experience is not repeated. It is the procedures which determine the success of an event, so they should be revisited, amended, followed, and never omitted for any reason.

The real solution to a complaint is to understand the cause of an issue. Then, adjust procedures to ensure that this issue cannot occur again. Eliminate the risk.

If a procedure can be tightened, it means the procedure was not tight enough. So, the complaint was legitimate.

AUTHOR'S VOICE BOX

There was a wedding where it became apparent on the day that the registrar had not been booked to officiate the legality of the marriage.

The only way to get around this was to continue with the wedding and conduct the ceremony with a guest playing the role of registrar.

The entire event was played out, including the ceremony, photographs, wedding breakfast, evening disco and buffet. The only thing missing was the registrar – which meant that the couple were not legally married.

The venue may not consider they were at fault because it is only the bride and groom who can book the registrar. Besides, the venue had asked the couple if they had booked the registrar and were assured they had.

198 POST-EVENT PROCEDURES

However, a venue has a responsibility to ensure that nothing can go wrong at an event. This is elimination of risk. So it is not enough to ask the couple, but the venue must check the evidence that the registrar has been booked.

Clients are allowed to be forgetful or unprofessional. But a venue is in the business of event management and is responsible for the success of the event. It must not rely on clients to do any part of the job – especially wedding clients, who might lack the skills and knowledge of events. It is the venue's responsibility to guide and advise their clients, and guarantee that nothing can go wrong with their most important day.

After this case, the venue revised its procedures to ensure that the situation could not happen again. This also suggests to me that the venue was at fault because if there was any room to amend their procedures, it seems the procedures were not tight enough beforehand.

Apart from the obvious problems with this situation, there is an issue of damage to the reputation of the venue. The couple are unlikely to tell everybody that it was their mistake. Additionally, the guests who attended will assume it was the venue's mistake.

All those guests will be talking about the wedding they attended at that venue which forgot to book the registrar and the couple had to pretend to be married!

27.4 Final report (Appendix IV)

Every event is a learning curve for whoever is involved in its planning and execution.

Whatever is learnt may be in the head, but brains do forget things – especially if the event does not recur for a year, or if a similar event occurs in three years' time. It is good practice, therefore, to make a record of the lessons from each event on a Final Report.

Appendix IV provides an example of a final report, but the main points to include are as follows.

- The venue manager's copy of the event schedule with notes, timing changes and checklist.
- A report of the objectives of the event and how each was met.
- A report of the venue debrief.
- A report of the client debrief.
- Notes on the client – their likes/dislikes/interests/personal notes.
- A list of suppliers involved with this event.
- Notes of what went particularly well.
- Notes of what did not go so well.
- Notes of any issues.
- Notes of any adjustments to procedures and the reasons.
- What to remember if this client were to rebook.
- What to remember if this event were to recur.

People move on to other jobs, so a professional venue manager would want the final report to provide information for anybody following in the same role. There is a legacy to consider after leaving one position for another, but also the venue will continue with its reputation and if it suffers in future it will not contribute to good standing on a curriculum vitae.

A venue must benefit from the learning, as well as the individual. The individual can take their learning to another job. The venue cannot do this and that should not be its disadvantage.

Also, if the client rebooks the venue it will be because the venue manager had made a success of the previous event. A professional venue manager will want his client to benefit from what went before.

The idea of the final report is that anybody in the future – including the same venue manager, of course – could get a good idea of what happened at that previous event.

This is valuable when a client rebooks or a similar event occurs and this document is retrieved in such cases. The final report can thus be placed into the new Client File to guide the venue manager through the process of planning the next event.

200 POST-EVENT PROCEDURES

Also, if an enquiry is received for a similar event, information on the final report can assist with responding to the enquiry or building the proposal – menus; costs; suppliers.

The final report is the last procedure of venue management and is the final document in the Client File. When this form is complete it closes the file. This is the true 'end' of an event.

Happy eventing!

Chapter 28

Case studies

CASE STUDY 1 by Philip Berners: the London Hippodrome

Venue

The London Hippodrome, Leicester Square, London, England

Profile

A large capacity venue for up to 1,000 guests in a high-profile location in Leicester Square at the centre of London's theatre, cinema and entertainment district.

In the 1980s, the venue was extremely successful as a nightclub under the stewardship of Peter Stringfellow and became the top London nightspot. Pop stars and celebrities of the day frequented the club, including Princess Diana.

After Stringfellow left the club in the 1990s, the London Hippodrome continued as a busy nightclub using its renowned name. It soon settled into being a lacklustre yet still very busy nightclub for foreign tourists.

Brief

My brief was to develop the opportunity of secondary income by hosting events during daytime hours when the nightclub was closed, and on slow trading nights, such as Mondays, Tuesdays and Wednesdays.

Negatives

Poor reputation; perception as an outdated nightclub which only tourists visit but Londoners do not. A venue that was known for being a nightclub, not an events venue. Key words: dated; seedy; tacky; dark.

Positives

Exciting location close to the Odeon for film premières. A recognisable landmark building. A large capacity venue. Impressive in-house sound and light systems. In-house projection. A hydraulic stage with lift launch. Car access from street to stage. Tiered auditorium. Balconies. Dance floor. Large backstage areas, kitchens and dressing rooms

Strategy

The management were entirely focused on the business of running a busy central London nightclub. But there was a need to differentiate between the venue trading as a nightclub and as a corporate venue.

The service to corporate clients needed to be rebranded, repackaged and launched to the corporate marketplace. Most especially, the handling of corporate clients needed to be professional.

Procedures were instigated that would meet the expectations and needs of corporate clients. These included the following.

- Direct phone line to the event manager's desk, so as to divert event enquiries from the untrained nightclub receptionist.

- New corporate stationery to differentiate the events department from the nightclub's profile.

- Reinvigorated attention to detail and cleanliness.

- Implementation of professional procedures, including enquiry handling and booking procedures, show-rounds, operational event management and standard operating procedures.

- Implementation of effective interdepartmental communication procedures.
- Repositioning of the brand extension at venue exhibitions.
- Introduction of promotion evenings to get potential clients into the venue and demonstrate the facilities and scope for corporate events.
- Design and print new corporate brochure with technical specifications and images of events.

Results

Success in the corporate event marketplace shed the old image and achieved the perception of the London Hippodrome as a serious venue for high-profile events.

Clients could rely on professionalism and dedication when they booked their event into the London Hippodrome.

The organisation culture shifted and all departments worked towards making corporate events successful.

The contribution to the core business increased from four events a year to over 100.

CASE STUDY 2   by Philip Berners: Thorpe Park

Venue

Thorpe Park, Surrey, England

Profile

A high-profile theme park west of London. The venue has water rides and rollercoasters, is the second most popular theme attraction in the UK and the tenth most visited theme park in Europe, with 1.9 million visitors per year.

The park covers 500 acres with six areas for private corporate hire.

Brief

To lead the events department, oversee the department's demerger from the entertainments department, grow the contribution from corporate events to the core business.

Negatives

Events was a division of the entertainments department, which diluted the emphasis of corporate events. Corporate events were run alongside the theme park, rather than as a standalone division. Resistance to events by many of the 600 staff. The theme park was closed during the winter months.

Positives

Opportunity to demerge the events department, restructure it and grow it. Attractions for corporate activities, events and fun days in situ. High-profile destination. Six areas available for corporate hire. Picturesque site. Celebrity attendance. Continual investment and upgrading of facilities. Extremely professional support departments, such as marketing and public relations.

Strategy

To reposition the events department and raise its profile, both internally among the management and staff, and externally to the corporate marketplace.

- Create an events division with direct phone lines, corporate stationery, dedicated catering and hospitable show-rounds.

- Extend the reach of Thorpe Park to local clients and London clients by exhibiting at international venue exhibitions.

- Extend the range of events, to include corporate fun days; barbecues; meetings; conferences; private hire evenings; trade fairs; Christmas craft fair; exhibitions; car shows; Christmas parties; boat shows on the lakes.

- Implementation of effective internal communications to integrate events with the staff that were affected by the alteration of daily park procedures.

Results

Significant growth of income from events. The increased contribution to the core business shifted the organisation culture and allowed more funding to be directed to the standalone events department.

Increased attention for events and funding allowed the development and increase of corporate venues within the theme park.

The shift in organisation culture changed the attitude of managers and staff, who began to embrace events.

The instigation of effective interdepartmental communication brought about a change in acceptance of corporate events.

The increase in creative and exciting events motivated the staff and management.

Significant growth of the events department and team.

The events department became the sole department to operate over the closed winter months, making events the only department bringing income into the business when the theme park was closed and otherwise not achieving revenue.

CASE STUDY 3 by Dimitri Lera: a wedding in Tuscany

Venue

La Cervara, Portofino, Tuscany, Italy

A key skill with venue management and organising events is the pedantic attention to detail. You've heard it before: details need to be checked, over and over again. This case study demonstrates how and why attention to detail is crucial.

One of the perks of organising events in Italy is the abundance of historical sites that are perfect venues for all sorts of events. This wedding was taking place in a former monastery at La Cervara on the western Ligurian coast, about half an hour's drive from Genoa, in Portofino.

The monastery was founded in 1361 and dedicated to San Girolamo. The prestige of San Girolamo della Cervara and its magnificent position made it the preferred destination of many illustrious personalities, whose visits are recorded in local journals. Items that form the décor have a high value, including rare books, artworks, tapestries and fine furniture. La Cervara monastery rests on a steep cliff overlooking the sea. It has been described as 'an epiphany for the spirit'.

I was in the position of food and beverage manager with a focus on events, and in this particular instance we were preparing an evening wedding dinner on the outside veranda of La Cervara. The veranda is large enough to seat 100 guests and overlooks the magnificent gulf of Portofino.

The event was taking place on a Saturday evening, as most weddings do in Italy. This allows for the event to carry on into the late hours, enabling guests to enjoy music, dancing and drinks surrounded by friends and the fantastic scenery, contributing to the memorable experience.

A converted abbey, the venue extends over three storeys. The veranda is on the ground floor with arched vaulted doors linking to a long corridor that runs the length of the entire building. On the first floor there is an adapted kitchen and a series of common rooms, including drawing rooms and a library. The second floor accommodates suites and apartments for overnight guests.

Unfortunately, the kitchen extractors had stopped working the week before the event. It was discussed whether to bring in a marquee to house a satellite kitchen, but this was deemed as an unnecessary expense – especially as the weather forecast confirmed clear weather and in Italy the weather is fairly reliable. Therefore, arrangements were made to house a satellite kitchen in the cloister at the back of the building, which was close enough to serve food to guests, but secluded enough for the fumes of the grilled dishes to disperse in the woods that border the cloister. It was thought to be the ideal solution.

The day of the event went well until a light wind brought a sudden shower. For my peace of mind, I went to check the drawing room upstairs. To my surprise, I noticed that smoke was quickly filling the room. Somebody from the chef brigade had opened a downstairs door in order for the smoke from the grilling to dissipate from the temporary kitchen, allowing it to drift upstairs. An antique book that smells like a steak loses its value very quickly! Some of the book covers are made of treated leather, and it takes a lengthy and costly procedure to eliminate unpleasant odours. Fortunately, I had entered the drawing room early enough to avoid any serious damage. I returned downstairs, closed the door and ensured that the chef brigade were informed of the problem and would not repeat the error.

This example shows the need to continually check all details and all areas of the venue during the event – not only during the planning and build stages. Just by the simple act of checking, I prevented major costly consequences.

Appendix I

Event forecast

Ten-day forecast from 8 March

DAY/TIME	NAME OF BOOKING	TYPE OF EVENT	ROOM	COVERS	FOOD REQ.	BEDROOMS	BOOKER DETAILS
8 March	David Foskett	Conference	Garden Suite	52	Day Delegate Package and working buffet lunch	52	David Foskett [email address]
14 March	Anita Cook	Charity Party	Ballroom	120	Banqueting Menu B 3 course sit-down	0	Anita Cook [phone number]

Appendix 11

Venue contract

Dated:

The Royal Hotel

AND

Client Name

Contact
For the Hire of Rooms, Services and Facilities
For [insert date of event]

THE ROYAL HOTEL – CONDITIONS OF TRADING

1 **Payment Terms**

    a   All prices quoted are exclusive of VAT which shall be payable at the rates ruling at the date of invoice.

    b   Unless otherwise agreed in writing, the Client shall pay the facility fee (being the charges for the hire of the venues, facilities and furnishings utilised for the event as detailed in Schedule A of this Agreement) on the signing of this Agreement or the date indicated as Final Payment Date on the Agreement. No booking will be accepted as confirmed by us unless this fee has been paid and the event will be cancelled with the full cancellation fees as detailed in this Agreement becoming payable to The Royal Hotel Country House Hotel.

    c   All accounts are payable within 14 days of receipt of invoice. Amounts invoiced must be paid in full without any set-off or counterclaim.

    d   Credit Accounts. Unless a credit facility has been granted to the Client, a pro-forma invoice will be issued estimating the final account covering all catering, entertainment and miscellaneous charges. This account must be settled in full at least 14 days prior to the event and if the account is not settled, the booking will be cancelled by us.

    e   Cancellation: In the event of cancellation of any booking by the Client, the Client shall pay a cancellation fee calculated as follows:

        i   For a one-day booking:

            a   the total amount due if notice of cancellation is received less than 10 days prior to the commencement of the function.

            b   50% of the total amount due if notice of cancellation is received between 28 days and 10 days prior to the commencement of the function.

            c   30% of the total amount due if notice of cancellation is received between 56 days and 28 days prior to the commencement of the function.

        ii   For a booking in excess of one day:

            a   The total amount due if notice of cancellation is received less than 60 days prior to the commencement of the total function.

            b   50% of the total amount due if notice of cancellation is received between 90 days and 60 days prior to the commencement of the function.

    c   30% of the total amount due if notice of cancellation is received between 120 days and 90 days prior to the commencement of the function.

Provided always that the amount of cancellation fees payable by the Client may be waived or reduced by us at our sole discretion.

2 **Catering Service**

THE ROYAL HOTEL does have its own catering facilities. In certain circumstances, THE ROYAL HOTEL may permit the client's preferred caterer to undertake catering but an additional charge will levied in these circumstances.

3 **Conditions**

    a   All our quotations are subject to availability on receipt of order.

    b   We do not accept any liability for any delays or cancellations arising as a result of:

        i   Strikes, riots or lock-outs affecting any of the trade in which we are concerned.

        ii   Exceptionally adverse weather conditions.

        iii   Loss or damage by fire or floods, or any other cause beyond our reasonable control.

        iv   Any Government or local authorities order or regulations including planning permission.

        v   Any circumstances beyond our reasonable control.

    c   Save in respect of liability for death or personal injury resulting from our negligence, our liability in respect of all claims arising in contract or tort shall be limited to the amount of the charges payable to us under such contracts.

    d   We shall not be liable in any circumstance for any indirect or consequential loss or damage whatsoever.

    e   The Client shall be responsible for the orderly conduct of any function and shall ensure that nothing shall be done which will constitute a breach of the law or in any way cause a nuisance or be infringement of or occasion or render possible forfeiture or endorsement of any licence for the sale of alcohol or for music and dancing.

    f   The Client shall indemnify us against all costs, charges, claims, expenses, demands and liabilities incurred by or made against us as a result of the negligence or wilful default of the Client or if its guests.

    g   The Client shall be responsible for any damage to ground or buildings caused by the erection of any temporary structure or by any vehicle or other equipment passing into the premises.

4 Access

Where THE ROYAL HOTEL is open to residents and the general public during the period of hire, vehicle access, external works and disruptive works will be restricted. All contractors will be required to comply with Health and Safety regulations.

Whilst the facilities listed are offered on an exclusive basis, the nature of the Hotel environment is such that some incidental noise and activity may over-spill into the contracted areas. Every reasonable precaution will be taken to ensure that any disruption is minimised.

5 Public Order Safety

The Client shall undertake:

    a   Not to obstruct any exit from or passage or gangway in the Building and the Premises nor to remove or otherwise interfere with any fire-fighting apparatus.

    b   Not without the previous written consent of THE ROYAL HOTEL to make or employ any additional lighting or extension from existing power sources or light fittings or any electrical gas or other appliance which requires compressed air, water or drainage. THE ROYAL HOTEL Technical Manager must be informed to supervise such arrangements.

    c   Not without the previous consent of THE ROYAL HOTEL to bring onto our use in the Building or the premises any explosive petroleum or radioactive material or any other item of noxious or dangerous nature.

    d   To notify The Management at THE ROYAL HOTEL immediately on becoming aware of any accident or injury occurring in the Building or Premises.

6 Publicity Material

The Client shall undertake:

    a   To submit the design and layout of all brochures (including advertisements) and all publicity material (including newspaper advertisements) for its prior approval, such approval not to be unreasonably withheld, THE ROYAL HOTEL reserves the right to stipulate the type and style of the words 'THE ROYAL HOTEL' as it is used in all such material.

b To use the THE ROYAL HOTEL logo in any publicity material but not so that such logo shall have greater emphasis on the remainder of the content of the publicity material.

c To produce all publicity material for the Function at its own cost. THE ROYAL HOTEL accepts no responsibility for promoting the Function.

d To indemnify THE ROYAL HOTEL against any loss claims or damages incurred by THE ROYAL HOTEL without limitation under the Consumer Protection Act 1987 arising out of the publication or issue of any publicity material not submitted by THE ROYAL HOTEL for approval in accordance herewith.

7 **Damage to Property**

The Client shall undertake to take all reasonable care of the Building and Premises and any property therein and to make good all damage and loss caused to the Building and Premises and any property therein (fair wear and tear and damage by insured risks excepted).

8 **Security**

THE ROYAL HOTEL maintains 24-hour duty management within the Premises, but does not offer specific arrangement for the safe keeping of the Client's displays and other equipment.

THE ROYAL HOTEL does not provide insurance cover for Client's or Clients Agents property and requires the Client to provide its own security and insurance arrangements for the event and the Client will provide details of such arrangements to THE ROYAL HOTEL at least 7 days before the commencement of the event.

THE ROYAL HOTEL accepts no liability for the loss, theft or damage to the Client's displays, technical and other equipment.

THE ROYAL HOTEL HEREBY AGREES AND UNDERTAKES AS FOLLOWS

1 **Service**

To provide the services contracted, which will include staffing and equipment necessary to service the function. In extreme cases, where by nature or size of the event or to expedite specific requests or requirements made by the Client, THE ROYAL HOTEL considers it desirable to provide additional staff, therefore THE ROYAL HOTEL shall be entitled to charge for such additional staff as a part of an additional service charge provided that all staff supplied in accordance with this sub-clause shall be under the direction and control of THE ROYAL HOTEL. THE ROYAL HOTEL will advise the Client of all such additional services and service charge prior to or at the time that they are incurred.

2 **Insurance**

To effect and maintain at its own cost:

a Material damage insurance in respect of the property of THE ROYAL HOTEL with insurance officers of repute against the risks of fire, storm, tempest, flood, explosion and burst pipes.

b Public liability insurance in respect of damage or injury caused by negligence of THE ROYAL HOTEL or its servants or employees or any other person undertaking at the building in connection with THE ROYAL HOTEL responsibilities under this Agreement to any of the Client's property or to any other persons whosoever, including visitors and other persons attending the Function.

3 **Public Order Safety**

To operate the premises in compliance with the Health and Safety at Work Act.

4 **Additional Staff**

If the Client shall request, THE ROYAL HOTEL shall use its best endeavours to provide any additional staff or specialist staff on request and THE ROYAL HOTEL shall be entitled to charge for such staff as part of the Service Charge.

5 Security

Notwithstanding anything contained herein, THE ROYAL HOTEL may for security purposes stop and search any persons entering the Building and shall be entitled to refuse to allow any person or thing to enter into the Building which it considers to be a risk to the safety or security of the Building or the persons therein and THE ROYAL HOTEL may in any case refuse admission to the Building to any person who is unable to present authority from the Client to enter the Building.

6 Conduct

THE ROYAL HOTEL may forbid or restrict any activity which it reasonably considers may be prejudicial to its interest in any way or to the interest of other persons entitled to use any part of the Building or may be offensive to individuals or groups against normal standard of decency likely to endanger order or safety.

7 'Per day' Hiring

'Per day' hiring constitutes 0800–1800 hours unless otherwise stated in the contract and hours outside these times may be charged at £200.00 per hour thereafter or part thereof at the discretion of the Management. No function will run past 2100 hours unless agreed in Schedule A. Set-up and de-rig hours will be agreed on Schedule A, where appropriate.

8 Variation of Agreement

This Agreement constitutes the entire Agreement of the parties and contains all the terms of this licence and may not be varied or added to except by written agreement signed by the parties or duly authorised parties on their behalf.

218 VENUE CONTRACT

Submitted to:

Submitted by:

SCHEDULE A – FURNISHINGS AND FACILITIES

Hire date:

Times: Get-in:

   Doors open:

   Event finish:

Venue hire: £

Venue hire includes:

Not included:

Payment terms:

Submitted to:

Submitted by:

SCHEDULE B – CATERING AND BAR REQUIREMENTS

220 VENUE CONTRACT

Submitted to:

Submitted by:

SCHEDULE C – ALL OTHER REQUIREMENTS

Submitted to:

Submitted by:

SCHEDULE D – TECHNICAL ARRANGEMENTS

Client to provide full technical specifications for any live performances to our Event Manager; liaise with Event Manager for any technical queries.

Appendix III

Function sheet/event schedule

Event: Murder Mystery Dinner

Date: Saturday 7 March 2015

Brief: 57 guests + 7 actors (Total 64)

DAY/TIME	ACTIVITY	WHO	CHECKED
Daytime	Garden Suite to be cleaned	Housekeeping	✓
Daytime	Garden Suite set up: • 8× round tables for 8 guests each • Table lay-up for 3 courses, coffee • Flower centrepieces • Novelty masks for each place • Place cards	Events	✓
18:00	Final venue check	Events	✓
18:30	Guests arrive to bar for complimentary cocktails	Reception / Bar	✓
19:00	Announcement for dinner	Events	✓ 5 mins late

19:05	Introduction	Actors
19:15	First course served	Events / Kitchen
19:30	Murder Mystery Act I	Actors
19:45	Second course served	Events / Kitchen
20:15	Murder Mystery Act II	Actors
20:45	Dessert course served	Events / Kitchen
21:00	Coffee served	Events
21:05	Murder Mystery Act III	Actors
21:30	End	
21:30	Guests move to lounge or bar	Bar
22:00	Garden Suite clear De-rig	Events

DISTRIBUTION: Reception / Kitchen / Bar / Garden Suite / Housekeeping / Event office

Appendix IV

Final report

EVENT DETAILS

Name of event:

Date of event:

Room:

Event organiser:

List of suppliers and contractors:

POSITIVE ASPECTS TO REMEMBER

(Venue / Suppliers / Timings / Pre-event management / Day-of-event management / Post-event management / Catering / Bars / Staffing / Access / Get-in / De-rig / Payments)

NEGATIVE ASPECTS TO REMEMBER

Glossary

Blackout Window blinds or coverings for glass roofs to block daylight from entering the venue. This is essential for daytime presentations or screenings that use projection. This is also necessary for the comfort of guests, so they do not get seated in direct sunlight.

Brown-field site A venue with basic facilities, such as a warehouse.

Corporate client A client representing a company or corporation, or where the company is paying the bill.

Dedicated event venue Venues built for the purpose of hosting events.

De-rig Dismantling all elements after an event has taken place.

Event schedule The detailed itinerary of an event.

Experiential (events) Events which appeal to a guest's senses: sight (theme and décor), sound (music and entertainment), touch (ambience), scent (food, fragrance), taste (food and drink).

Final walk-round The last venue check on the day of an event, before the doors open and guests enter the venue.

Function sheet See *Event schedule*.

Get-in The contractual time of access to a venue.

Get-out The contractual time of exit from a venue – when the venue must be clear.

Green-field site A venue with no facilities, such as parkland or a disused building.

Guest experience (The) Everything a guest experiences during an event.

Heads of Department (HODs)   Departmental managers of a venue.

Lead-in   The time between receiving confirmation from a client, and the date of the event – the planning stage.

Meal experience (The)   Everything a diner experiences during a meal.

Non-dedicated event venue   Venues built for a purpose other than events – where their core business is not events, and where events are not the main revenue stream.

Private client   Individual client(s), such as the bride and groom for a wedding.

Raked seating   Tiered seating.

Recce (reconnaissance)   A visit to view a venue (see *Show-round*).

Running order   See *Event schedule*.

Show-round   When a client visits a venue to view it before deciding to book.

Sight line   View to the stage.

Special venues   Venues which are unusual and would not usually host an event.

Strike/striking   Clearing elements after an event.

Turn-around   Changing the set-up of a room, so as to use it for another purpose.

Unusual venues   See *Special venues*.

Index

Locators in **bold** indicate tables and sample documents.

access to event areas: security briefing 176; venue contract 150–151, **216**
accommodation, hotels as venues 13, 14, 15–16
account managers *see* client account managers
advice to client: catering outlets 75–77; date conflicts 138–139; event managers 65–69; external services 87–90; show-round 145
appearance of venue: marketing 95; professionalism 33, 35
areas *see* access to event areas
attracting clients *see* winning business

bars 83–84
booker's evenings 97–98
bookings *see* confirmation procedures; enquiry handling; lead-in procedures; winning business
branding, hotels as venues 15, 16–17; *see also* marketing
briefings: with client 51, 194–198; debriefs 189–191, 194–198; during-event procedures 175–176; security 176; with sponsors 51–52; venue culture change 49–50
BRIT Awards 152
budgets 105; creation of 109–112; development of 112–114; discount on the bill 181, 196; low-budget events 12, 13, 118–119; origination of 106–109; return on investment (ROI) 114–118; unusual venues 19; venue hire fee 118–119; *see also* events as a source of income
buffet service 127–128

cable trip hazards 129
cafes 83–84
cancellation procedures 150
capacity of venue 92–95, **95**, 153
careers, events management 30–31
case studies: London Hippodrome 96, 201–203; Thorpe Park, Surrey 26, 203–205; Tuscany wedding 205–207
catering *see* food and drink
catering outlets 74–87
chain hotels 15
charges for venues: budgets 118–119; confirmation procedures 149–150; reactive marketing 93; *see also* events as a source of income
cheap events *see* low-budget events
checking (monitoring): debriefs 195–196; during-event procedures 179–180; final walk-round 125–126, 144, 176–178
children, buffet service safety 127

230   INDEX

cleanliness 34–35, 129–130
client account managers: hotels as venues 12–13; one-person management structure 55–62
client briefings 51
client debrief 190–191, 194–198
client file procedures 158–159
client portfolio 21
client relationship: checking expectations are being met 180; debriefs 190–191, 194–198; lead-in period 156–157, 160–162; one-person management structure 57–58, 162; post-event procedures 190–191, 194–198; show-round 23; *see also* advice to client; professionalism
client relationship procedures 160–162
client retention 102–104, 194
clients: budget setting 106–109; debrief meeting 190–191, 194–198; as event organisers 63, 64–65; lead-in period 156–157; meeting expectations 41–42; one-person management structure 57–58, 59–60; and professionalism 23, 37; show-round 142–145; trust 98–99, 145; venue choice 92–95; weddings 88–90; *see also* advice to client
cloakrooms 128–129, 179
closing events: de-rig procedures 183–184; during-event procedures 181–182; *see also* post-event procedures
common mistakes *see* pitfalls
communication: interdepartmental 46–52; problem solving 194–198; venue culture change 44–54; *see also* briefings
complaints: client debrief 190–191, 196–198; food and drink 180–181; legal context 191; legitimacy 181; post-event procedures 196–198
concerts, catering outlets 81–82
conferences, catering outlets 84–86
confidentiality 152

confirmation procedures 146–153, 160
contact lists 165
contact point *see* one-person management structure
contract catering 78–80
contract procedures 146–153, **213–223**
costs *see* budgets; charges for venues
creativity, hotels as venues 11–12
culture *see* venue culture change

dates: confirmation procedures 147; conflicts 138–139; event schedules 166
debriefs 189–191, 194–198
dedicated venues 3–4, **4, 5**; events as a source of income 24–25; one-person management structure 50, 61; professionalism 29
delegate rates 17
departmental divisions 46–52
de-rig procedures 183–184; *see also* post-event procedures
dining *see* food and drink
discount on the bill 181, 196
DJs 89–90
doors opening 125–126
during-event procedures 175–176; checking 179–180; closing 181–182; final walk-round 176–178; food and drink 180–181; opening the doors 125–126, 177, 178; pitfalls in meeting guest expectations 124–131; security briefing 176

ending of event *see* closing events; de-rig procedures; post-event procedures
enquiry handling 135–137; date conflict 138–139; file procedure 140–141; one-person management structure 60; professionalism 35; receipt of 138
entrance area 124–125, 178–179
evaluation, guest satisfaction 192–194; *see also* complaints; feedback

INDEX

event co-ordinators 56; *see also* event organisers
event forecasts 47–48, **209–210**
event needs, hierarchy of 8–10, 14
event organisers: advice to client 65–69; briefing meetings 49–50; budgets 105; hotels as venues 12–13, 15–16; meeting expectations 41–42; professionalism 37, 38–40; show-round 23; three types of 63–65
event schedules *see* function sheets; schedules
event types 22, 25
event venue managers: budgets 105; client portfolio 21; during-event procedures 178–182; enquiry handling 138; as event organisers 63–65; events as a source of income 24, 25; external services 87–90; hierarchical structure 55–57; lead-in period 156–157; meeting expectations 41–42; one-person management structure 55–62, 135, 162; onsite event management 58–62; operational procedures 168–169; post-event procedures 188–191; professionalism 36, 37, 38–40; promotion evenings 97–98; qualifications 19–20; rehearsal procedures 173–174; role of the venue 70–73, 72–73; show-round 142–145; types of event 22; understanding client experience 65–69; venue culture change 51; *see also* advice to client
events, definition 3
events as a source of income: as primary source 24–25; as secondary source 25–28; value of event 50; *see also* budgets
expectations *see* meeting expectations
expenditure *see* budgets; charges for venues
experience of staff: event organisers 64–69; professionalism 29–30; reputation 18–19; understanding client experience 65–69

external services 74–77; advice to client 87–90; approved external providers 75–77; catering outlets 74–87; pitching 101–102

facilities, venue contracts 151, **218**
feedback: guest satisfaction evaluation 192–194; reputation 20–21; *see also* complaints
fees *see* budgets; charges for venues
final reports 198–200, **224–225**
final walk-round (before event) 125–126, 144, 176–178
finances *see* budgets; charges for venues; events as a source of income
flow of guests 124–125, 178–179
food and drink: buffet service 127–128; contract procedures 153, **215**; during-event procedures 180–181; external services 74–87; hotels as venues 14, 17; one-person management structure 59–60; welcome drinks 124–125
force majeure 151–152
forthcoming events *see* event forecasts
freelance event managers 63, 64–65, 68–69
function sheets 48–49, 163–166, **211–212**

get-in procedures 171–172; *see also* opening the doors
'good' venues, professionalism 34–38
greeting guests 130–131
guest experience: common mistakes 124–131; evaluation and feedback 192–194; food and drink 180–181; meeting expectations 41–42; as priority 120; and professionalism 31–32, 37
guests at venues: capacity of venue 92–95, **95**; de-rig procedures 183–184; hire contract 153; personal safety 120–122; risk management 122–124
guidance *see* advice to client

232 INDEX

head of events **56**, 56–57, **57**; see also event venue managers
heads of department (HOD) meetings 52–54
hierarchy of event needs 8–10, 14
Highclere Castle, Berkshire 27–28
Hilton, Paris 42
hire contract 146–153
hire periods 147–148
history of a venue 20
hosts, greeting guests 131
hotels as venues 11–17
housekeeping 34–35, 129–130

income see budgets; events as a source of income
indemnity 152
information management, one-person 58
in-house catering 74–77
insurance **218**
itinerary 149; see also function sheets; schedules

lead-in procedures 154–155; client relationship 156–157, 160–162; period of time 155–157
legacy of event 187, 199–200
legal context: contract procedures 146–153; role of the venue 72; safety 121, 122
liability 152
lighting, risk management 123
likeability: lead-in period 156–157; repeat business 102–103; show-round 23; see also client relationship
live happenings 3
logistics: date conflicts 138–139; operational procedures 167–170
London Fashion Week 28
London Hippodrome 96, 201–203
longer-term contracts 103–104
low-budget events: charges for venues 118–119; hotels as venues 12, 13

Madame Tussauds 28
managers see event venue managers

marketing: hotel branding 15, 16–17; hotels as venues 13–17; proactive 96–98; reactive 91–96; testimonials 20–21; venue contracts **216–217**; winning events business 98–99; word of mouth referrals 22
meeting expectations: checking expectations are being met 180; debriefs 190–191, 194–198; guest experience 41–42; see also complaints; feedback
meetings, location of 156–157; see also briefings
meetings as events, catering outlets 84–86
Milan Fashion Week 139
mirrors, cloakrooms 129
mistakes see pitfalls
monitoring see checking
multi-purpose venues see non-dedicated venues
museums: events as a source of income 28; venue culture change 43

noise issues 143
non-dedicated venues 4–5, **5, 6**; diversifying range of events 25; events as a source of income 24–28; good communication 44–46; hotels 11–17; one-person management structure 50, 61; professionalism 29; promotion evenings 97–98; staff experience 18–19; unusual venues 6–7; venue culture change 43–44

'on the day' see during-event procedures
one-person management structure 55–57; client relationship 57–58, 162; disseminating information 58; enquiry handling 135; onsite event management 58–62; receiving information 58
online reviews 21
onsite event management, one-person 58–62; see also during-event procedures; post-event procedures

INDEX 233

onsite logistics 167–170
opening the doors 125–126; during-event procedures 178; final walk-round 125–126, 177; timing 125, 178
operational procedures 167–170
organisers *see* event organisers; event venue managers
overnight accommodation, hotels as venues 13, 14, 15–16
overtime 43–44

Party in the Park event 27
payment terms 149–150, **214–215**
people *see* clients; event organisers; event venue managers; guests at venues; staff; suppliers
personal safety *see* safety
personalities: lead-in period 156–157; show-round 23, 142; *see also* client relationship
pitching 100–102
pitfalls: guests at venues 124–131; one-person management structure 60; professionalism 18–19, 29–30
portfolio of clients 21
post-event procedures 187–189; debriefs 189–191, 194–198; final report 198–200; guest satisfaction 192–194; problem solving 194–198; *see also* de-rig procedures
pre-event briefings 49–50
proactive marketing 96–98
problem solving 194–198
procedures for event handling 35–38; *see also* client file procedures; client relationship procedures; confirmation procedures; de-rig procedures; during-event procedures; enquiry handling; function sheets; get-in procedures; lead-in procedures; operational procedures; rehearsal procedures; set-up procedures; show-round
procurement *see* external services
professionalism 29–34; enquiry handling 139; get-in procedures 171–172; 'good' venues 34–38;
opening the doors 126; repeat business 102–103; reputation 18–19, 32, 36; salesy approach 40, 144–145; show-round 38–40; trust 98–99
profits *see* budgets; charges for venues; events as a source of income; value of event
promotion evenings 97–98
provisional bookings 140–141
purpose-built venues *see* dedicated venues

qualifications of staff 19
queuing: buffet service 127–128; opening the doors 126

rapport *see* client relationship
reactive marketing 91–96
referrals 22; *see also* repeat business
rehearsal procedures 173–174
relationships *see* client relationship; venue culture change
repeat business 102–104, 194
reputation 18–20; client portfolio 21; event managers 64; external services 74, 75, 90; history of a venue 20; legacy of event 187; online reviews 21; post-event procedures 194, 196; professionalism 18–19, 32, 36; role of the venue 70–72; show-round 23; testimonials 20–21; by type of event 22; word of mouth referrals 22
Request for Information (RFI) 99
Request for Proposal (RFP) 100
response to client needs 35; *see also* client relationship; professionalism
responsibility for event 170
restaurants, as catering outlets 83–84
restrooms 129–130
retention of business 102–104, 194
return on investment (ROI) 114–118
revenue *see* budgets; charges for venues; events as a source of income
reviews 20–21; *see also* reputation
risk assessments 123–124

risk elimination, service delivery 197–198
risk management 122–124, 182; see also safety
role of the venue 63–73, 90
running order 48–49; see also function sheets; itinerary

safety: buffet service 127–128; during-event procedures 182; final walk-round 125–126, 176–178; guests at venues 120–122; risk management 122–124, 182; terrorism 86–87; trip hazards 129; venue contracts **216**
sales: pitching 100–101; professionalism 40, 144–145; reputation 20; show-round 144–145; see also marketing
schedules: checking and adjustments 179–180; cloakrooms 128; function sheets 48–49, 163–166, **211–212**; get-in procedures 171–172; hire periods 147–148; itinerary 149; lead-in period 154–157; opening the doors 125–126; set-up procedures 172; welcome drinks 124–125; see also dates; during-event procedures
security: briefing meetings 176; external services 86–87; greeting guests 130–131; venue contracts **217, 219**
self-regulation 19–20
services: lead-in period 155–157; promotion evenings 97–98; venue contracts 151, **218**
set-up procedures 172
show-round: enquiry handling **136**, 136–137; procedures for event handling 142–145; professionalism 38–40; promotion evenings 97–98
small events, catering outlets 84–86
sound equipment 66–67, 69–71
sponsor briefings 51–52
stadiums, catering outlets 81–82
staff: briefings 49–50, 175–176; careers 30–31; communication process 52–54; enquiry handling 135, 138; experience and shortfalls 18–19; hierarchical structure 55–57, **56, 57**; interdepartmental communication 46–52; qualifications 19; show-round 23; venue contracts 151, **218**; venue culture change 43–46; venue debrief 189–190; see also professionalism
start see opening the doors
suppliers see external services

team at venue see staff
technical expertise: catering outlets 80; hotels as venues 17; sound equipment 66–67, 69–71; venue choice 95–96
temporary nature of events, safety 121
tendering 99–100
terrorism 86–87
testimonials 20–21; see also reputation
Thorpe Park, Surrey 26, 203–205
timing see dates; schedules
toilets 129–130
trade fairs 96–98
traditional venues see dedicated venues
training of staff 29–30
trip hazards 129
trust 98–99, 145
turn-arounds 184
Tuscany wedding case study 205–207
types of event 22, 25

unusual venues 6–7; demand for 7; hierarchy of event needs 9–10; staff experience 18–19; types of event 22

value of event 50; see also events as a source of income
venue choice 92–95; see also winning business
venue contracts 146–153, **213–223**
venue culture change 43–44; communication process 52–54; good communication 44–46; interdepartmental communication 46–52

venue exhibitions 96–98
venue hire fee *see* charges for venues
venue managers *see* event venue managers
venue recce *see* show-round
venue reputation *see* reputation
venues: definition 3; role of 63–73, 90; types overview 3–7; *see also* dedicated venues; non-dedicated venues; unusual venues
versatility of venue 94, 95, 97–98
viewing the venue *see* show-round
visits *see* show-round

walk-round *see* final walk-round (before event); show-round
wash-up *see* post-event procedures
wedding fairs 98
weddings: complaints 197–198; external services 88–90; Tuscany case study 205–207
welcome drinks 124–125
welcomes, greeting guests 130–131
wind-down period *see* closing events
winning business 91; charges for venues 118–119; in events 98–99; pitching 100–102; proactive marketing 96–98; reactive marketing 91–96; show-round 142–145, 161; tendering 99–100; *see also* client retention
word of mouth referrals 22

zoo, venue culture change 46, 50–51